OFF TO WAR

Stories of Ilkeston & District
soldiers, sailors and airmen
1914-1918

By Grant Shaw

**In memory of all those from Ilkeston and District
who served their country in the First World War
and of all those who waited for them at home**

For Henry Shaw (1894-1916)
and Henry Shaw (1931-2009)

Ilkeston & District Local History Society 2014
Second Edition 2015

ISBN 978 0902165 26 7

Published by
Ilkeston and District Local History Society
www.ilkestonhistory.org.uk

Pagination and Print Management by:

tel: 0115 932 0643 web: www.moorleys.co.uk

The author would like to give special thanks to his good friend and collaborator Paul Miller, whose help and advice both at home and abroad have made producing this book a much easier task.

The Society also thanks the many others who helped with this project, particularly:

Marion Axford
Bablake School
Mike Baker
Janet Barlow
Granville Biggin
Glennis Bird
Betty Butelli
John Chapman
Marina Charlton
Commonwealth War Graves
    Commission
Anne Cook
Danny Corns
Erewash Museum
Ann Featherstone
Stephen Flinders
Friends of Park Cemetery
John & Jenifer Giblin
Sheila Gillott
Megan Grace
Sara Hamilton
Hazel Hartshorn
Gary Henshaw
David Hudson
Ilkeston Advertiser

Ilkeston Library
Ilkeston Life Magazine
Imperial War Museum
Malcolm Jarvis
Beverley Kilby
David Kirk
Tony Leivers
Ken Mather
National Archives
Jack Naylor
Marion Newbold
Paul Opiah
Picture the Past
Ian Quinn
Margaret Richardson
Royal British Legion
Brian Spiby
Michael Talbot
Kath Trueman
Bryan Turner
Phil Tyler
Nora Waite
Dolores Watson
Worksop College

We would also like to thank the following for their help with the expanded second edition:

Christine Allen
Lily Barker
Angela Carlin
Don Boden Chambers
Joe Ellaby
Colin Greaves

Anne Hadfield
Linda McKay
Pete Pheasant
Joyce Rich
Eric Saunders

An unidentified Lance Corporal in the Sherwood Foresters, possibly at Annual Camp before the War.
He wears crossed rifles on his left sleeve indicating he is a marksman and probably served
his time in the regular Army before joining the 'Territorials'.

OFF TO WAR

THEIR NAME LIVETH FOR EVERMORE

Grant Shaw

ABOUT THIS BOOK

When we think of the First World War - 'The Great War' to those who came through it - most of us think of trenches, machine guns and seas of mud in France or Belgium.

Certainly most of the men from Ilkeston and District who went to war from 1914 to 1918 did fight in Picardy and Flanders and many of them are still there, but local men also fought at sea – on one of the first Royal Navy ships to be lost in that war and on one of the last. Ilkeston men also died at Jutland in the major sea battle of the war and fought the enemy at Tsingtao in China and in the Rufiji River in Tanzania. Many sailors and Marines served on the Western Front and at Gallipoli in the Royal Naval Division, which fought alongside the army in similarly awful conditions. Men from both services transferred to the Royal Flying Corps. Some volunteered for the medical services and helped their wounded comrades in all theatres of the war.

Men from Ilkeston fought Bulgarians in Macedonia and the Ottoman Empire in Palestine, Syria and what is now Iraq. They also fought alongside the Italians in Austria and in Slovenia. Some were old hands who had served in the Army or Navy for years, others keen volunteers or raw conscripts with no battle experience whatever. They died by accident or disease as well as by enemy action and a surprising number made it back to an often difficult homecoming, trying to re-adapt to domestic life with varying success.

It is not possible to record in this book the stories of all those who fought in the war who had an Ilkeston connection, as there are so many and sadly for some their stories and service records have been lost in the century which followed. Ilkeston's sombre Cenotaph does not contain all their names, nor indeed is it easy to find an Ilkeston connection for everyone mentioned on it.

To do proper justice to them all would require many years of effort and resources which are not available to volunteers from a Local History Society. Instead, we hope that this random selection of stories, photographs and other memorabilia may serve as a small gesture of our appreciation for the incredible sacrifices made by those from Ilkeston and the surrounding area who fought in the First World War, whether or not they came back to tell their story.

Ilkeston & District Local History Society
May 2014

PREFACE TO THE SECOND EDITION

Since the First Edition was published we have been contacted by more family members with further stories and images to share, and so we have taken the opportunity to expand the book to include as many of these as possible. Since the centenary in August 2014 we have all seen many commemorations of the sacrifices made by people during the Great War and it is the least we can do to try to preserve the memory of as many of those who fought in it as we can.

IDLHS, January 2015

Bath Street dressed up for the visit of the King and Queen, June 1914.

Reserve soldiers parading for the Royal visitors, Ilkeston Market Place, June 1914.

Chapter One

ILKESTON ON THE EVE OF WAR

In the last weekend of June 1914, the people of Ilkeston were too concerned with the great honour done to the district by the visit of King George V and Queen Mary only the previous Thursday for very much notice to be taken of the assassination of Archduke Francis Ferdinand of Austria-Hungary and his wife in Sarajevo on Sunday June 28th. Indeed, this event is hardly mentioned at all by the next several issues of the Ilkeston newspapers (the Pioneer and the Advertiser), which like most local papers at that time contained a page or two of national and international news.

The Ilkeston Pioneer of Friday June 26th contains a 'full description of the proceedings' of the first official Royal visit to the Borough of Ilkeston.

"The people of Ilkeston living along the line of the route taken by the King and Queen ... responded splendidly to the request to decorate their houses, and in the main business arteries the tradesmen lost no opportunity of expressing their loyalty in the adornment of their establishments ... at night the illuminations in certain cases were extremely good. ... The Market Place had much decoration bestowed upon it both by the Corporation and private residents ... Soon after one o'clock the Market Place began to assume an appearance of great animation and life when the school children commenced to arrive in their processions. At the same time the large staff of police under the orders of Capt. Holland (Chief Constable of Derbyshire) was distributed over the route with Sergeant Walker and Inspector Holmes in general charge. Altogether 300 extra police were brought into the town and the full local force of thirty were on duty ...

By two o'clock the Ilkeston Branch of the National Reserve, numbering over 200 men, marched into the square, headed by their band, the men of whom were hardly recognisable in their smart new uniforms with silver facings ... some of these men had fought in famous campaigns; one, Caleb Wood, being one of the survivors from the terrible night at Rorke's Drift during the Zulu War. Almost simultaneously there arrived the band of the 5th Battalion (Sherwood Foresters) Notts and Derby Regiment, under their Drum Major. Then came the men of the Ilkeston and Long Eaton Company of the 5th Battalion (Territorials) in their scarlet uniforms, with fixed bayonets, to act as a Guard of Honour for the King. Capt. Newton was in command ... The Company were headed on their march from Headquarters by the Special Reserve Band from the Derby Depot, who were also accompanied by the 5th Battalion Drum and Bugle Band ...

Long before three o'clock the Market Place was well filled with people, and the scene was one of marvellous colour and interest. The special stands in the churchyard were well filled, and even on the church tower there were people, presumably the ringers, ready to welcome the King with a peal of bells. Every window commanding a view of the scene was filled with people, and the windows and balcony of the Town Hall were all occupied. All eyes were turned on the grandstand ... it was an imposing structure occupying the whole of the Town hall front ... the front had been draped in royal purple and white relieved by gold bands and fringe.

The pavilion built for the royal reception was particularly handsome ... the front was carpeted in scarlet, and on either side of the steps up which Royalty was to pass there was a fine group of pot flowers and plants ... The Duke and Duchess of Rutland arrived on the scene in good time ... the arrival of Col. Seely was specially noted by the children, who vigorously waved their flags in recognition of the Member [of Parliament] for the Division.

The King was just a few minutes late ... the bells rang out a merry peal while the children cheered long and loudly. The prearranged signal of his Majesty reaching the Junction was a blast from the siren at the Cossall Colliery ... the Royal car slowly came into the square ... the military salute was given and the guests in the pavilion and grandstand rose to greet the King ... following the Royal car with the King and Queen were others, in one of which was the Duke of Portland, whose guest his Majesty is this week ... They were accompanied by the Archbishop of York, who had travelled with the suite from Welbeck.

The Mayor of Ilkeston (Coun. J.A. Macdonald) in gold chain and robe, was in the pavilion ready to receive their Majesties, and with him was the Mayoress ... King George wore a lounge suit and the familiar brown bowler, and the Queen was gowned in dark blue ninon lightly draped over white with cerise flowered hat. On the steps of the pavilion his Grace of Portland introduced his Majesty to the Mayor and then presented Col. Seely ... the formal presentations followed ...

Though Coun. F.P. Sudbury was the last to be presented to the King, he was not the least, for as Chairman of the Governors of the County Secondary School he asked his Majesty graciously to open the handsome new premises at Pimlico by pressing an electric button in the pavilion. Mr Bellamy, the manager of the Tramway and Electricity Department, was ready with a specially prepared table, and the King pressed the button. The message flashed to the County School, where the current operated an electric lock and liberated the latch. A carefully prepared spring at once pulled the doors open, and the success of the ceremony was signalled by the firing of a bomb ... his Majesty had a time table to observe, and he and the Queen moved towards their waiting car, while the children cheered again and again, and the band played the National Anthem. His Majesty gave a final bow to the Mayor and Mayoress and the ladies and gentlemen in the pavilion, and the car moved on. He did not forget, however, to give a kindly nod to the battle veterans lined up by the pavilion ...

Leaving Wharncliffe Road, the Royal cortege passed down leafy Pimlico Lane [West End Drive] by the Mayor's residence, and then through the new avenue by the new secondary schools [King George Avenue]. Here their Majesties had a view of the scholastic institution the King had a few minutes before ceremoniously opened by pressing a button.

Contrary to expectation, the Royal car stopped at the gates of the school, his Majesty's attention having no doubt been called by the Duke of Portland to the Headmaster, Mr F.P.C. Walker M.A., who was there with his staff and pupils. Mr Walker was presented by Lord Stamfordham [the King's Private Secretary] and the King shook hands with him ...

The final scenes in Ilkeston's thirty minutes greeting of the King were enacted as the Royal car passed through Lord Haddon Road, Pelham Street and Bath Street to Heanor Road. At the

Above : The Market Place dressed in readiness for the King's visit in June 1914.
Below : The Army Reserve parading under very different circumstances a few weeks later.

Ilkeston Hospital a green flag was exhibited, and the speed of the motors was increased as their Majesties left the Borough and proceeded towards Heanor. Telephone message reached us at Ilkeston from the Police that the King crossed the boundary into Notts. at 4.10pm and during the Derbyshire portion of his tour there were no occurrences to mar the success of the Royal progress."

By the following Pioneer issue of 30th June, the news was still of the Royal Visit, with a small, polite criticism in the Editorial that the events had been "just a little over-programmed", meaning that too much had been planned for the time available, and that the "accommodation for the pressmen and photographers was inadequate".

The Advertiser reported that some national newspapermen had been carping about the facilities accorded to them (they were caught up with the crowd) but the Pioneer said that the Mayor and Councillors "were not to blame as, as far as could be established their wish had been for every facility to be given" to the Pressmen. Presumably this accounts for the lack of good quality photographs of the occasion. Praise was given to the King for literally going out of his way to see the new school he had opened remotely and the suggestion was made that the local MP, Col. Seely had encouraged this to His Majesty.

Ilkeston's Territorial (part time) soldiers along with the rest of their brigade, were by the beginning of August in annual training at Hunmanby Camp, near Filey, close to the Yorkshire coast. Although the weather had been inclement, there was no fear of the camp being flooded, said the Pioneer. "The battalions are disposed in formations exactly like a capital 'T'", the cross stroke including the local 5th Battalion whose strength was said to be 920.

A CALL TO ARMS

The Pioneer of August 7th reports "GREAT BRITAIN AT WAR - Germany defies Europe" and gives a summary of the very complicated series of events which had led to it.

Author's Note : Hundreds if not thousands of books have been written about how and why the Great War started - and this is not one of them. If you would like a detailed account of the years leading up to the war and the several times war almost broke out before 1914 I can recommend Professor Margaret MacMillan's recent book 'The War That Ended Peace: The Road to 1914'.

ILKESTON'S TERRIERS MOBILISED (Ilkeston Pioneer)

The Territorial Army camp near Filey had been recalled the previous Monday, with Ilkeston and Long Eaton's 'G' Company receiving orders to strike camp at about 8.30am, while they were "Disporting themselves in the briny". They entrained in the early hours of Tuesday morning, reaching Ilkeston at about 8.15am.

The men, many of whom remained in uniform throughout the day, received an order for mobilisation (by which they were officially 'called up') that same evening. Ilkeston's Terriers fell in at the Drill Hall on Stanton Road at nine o'clock on Wednesday morning, with arms and full equipment, watched by "a large and excited assembly". The number on parade was 182. Capt. H. Newton was in command. "The men were first medically inspected by Dr Powell of Ilkeston, and a kit inspection and drill followed. Each man had received instructions to bring food for one day, and it was stated that breakfast on Thursday morning would be provided for those accommodated at the Drill Hall all night". While waiting, the men "displayed the utmost good spirit. Cries of 'are we downhearted?' met with a voiciferous reply of 'No'" said the Pioneer. The men were told that the majority of them would return to their homes for the night and reassemble the following morning (Thursday). They were to march to Derby about ten o'clock and await further orders there. The Pioneer continued :

"Enthusiastic scenes marked the departure of the Ilkeston company on Thursday morning. The men were addressed in the Drill Hall by Capt. Newton and then formed up and marched through a cheering avenue of spectators to White Lion Square. Here they were received by the Mayor of Ilkeston (Coun. J.A. Macdonald) and the Corporation in civic state [...] Speaking to the fine body of men before him, the Mayor said that on this very historic occasion it was only fitting that the Mayor and Corporation of the Borough should attend to wish the local Territorials 'God Speed'. This great country of theirs was at war, a war not of their own seeking, but England always stepped in to defend the weak against a tyrant and an aggressor (cheers). The Citizens of Ilkeston and its sister town of Long Eaton were proud of those men who in time of peace had come forward and train themselves to defend their country in the hour of need and, if necessary, would go into foreign fields to defend the weak. May the war be short, and may they come back triumphant and the country God had made great come out greater still. He wished them God Speed and said that if any of them held misgivings for the safety of those they had left behind, he would assure them that the citizens of that borough would not see them want (cheers). 'God speed to you' said the Mayor, 'All honour and glory be yours'.

"Capt. Newton, replying, said for them [sic] that was a proud yet solemn moment. Wherever they went, their motto would be 'For King and Country'. They all believed in the justice of their cause, and they all would stand shoulder to shoulder. He commended to the Mayor and the citizens the care of the wives and families whom some of the men were leaving behind. They would all strive hard to hold high the fair names of Ilkeston and Long Eaton (applause). Rousing cheers were raised for the officers and men, and they replied with a counter demonstration for the Mayor and the town. To the accompaniment of farewell cheers the men marched away via Stanton Road, Kirk Hallam and Locko Park to their Derby Headquarters".

The Borough Council Minutes report that members of the Council then returned to the Town Hall and the Mayor (Councillor J.A. Macdonald) donated the sum of £70, being the balance of the sum which had been granted to him in recognition of his work on the Royal visit, and a balance of £70 from the 'Coal Strike Distress Fund' to form a fund for "alleviating distress among the wives and families of persons called to the colours". The jobs of all Corporation

The army buying horses in Burgin's Yard, off South Street in Ilkeston in August 1914
Below : The purchased horses are led off.

employees would be kept open for them and during their period of service their full pay, less their pay from HM Government, would be paid to their dependants.

The Ilkeston Pioneer reports "HORSES FOR THE FRONT

On Friday a great number of horses from Ilkeston and district paraded before Major Leach and a veterinary inspector, in the Corporation Yard, Pimlico and those selected were branded with the government mark.

The selected animals, many of them fine specimens of horseflesh, were assembled before a big crowd about mid-day on Saturday at the rear of the Free Library. Here they were finally inspected and cheques in payment handed to the owners by Major Leach.

Shortly before two o'clock a detachment of the South Notts Hussars marched into the square, carrying full riding equipment, and the process of saddling was witnessed with the greatest interest. Some of the horses were affected by the strangeness of the procedure, but they eventually settled down and behaved as military horses should. [...] It is highly probable by this time that many of them are with the Hussars in Norfolk".

"ILKESTON SCOUT WITH THE COLOURS

Patrol Leader J.W. Moore, aged 18, of the 1st Ilkeston Company of Boy Scouts, offered at Wednesday Morning's mobilisation to accompany the local Territorials to whatever destination they were bound. He will act as a bugler. Moore's home is at 4, Wilton Place".

Note : John William Moore joined the 1st/5th Sherwood Foresters in Derby on 8th August 1914 (the day after the above article was published), aged 18 years 3 months. He made it through the war and died aged 74 in 1970.

"POLICE AND TRAMWAYMEN WITH THE FORCES

Police Constable Hill, of Ilkeston, a member of the Fleet Reserve, received orders on Monday morning to report for duty at once. Police Constables Irwin, Chawner, and Owen, Army reservists, were also recalled for duty. Each man was presented with a pipe and four ounces of tobacco, subscribed for by the officers and men of the Ilkeston Constabulary. Another local policeman to rejoin his regiment is P.C. Dodd, of Ilkeston Junction.

Tramway Inspector Burbidge left on Wednesday morning to join the Royal Army Medical Corps at Netley near Southampton and on the same morning Motorman Hinton departed for duty with the Army Service Corps at Aldershot" (See entry for former PC George Irwin, known as 'Ilkeston's first casualty').

"COL. SEELY'S COMMISSION

The 'London Gazette' on Friday night announced that Col. J.E.B. Seely DSO, MP, the Member [of Parliament] for the Ilkeston Division, [...] has been called to the colours".

Author's Note : John Edward Bernard ("Galloper Jack") Seely, later first Baron Mottistone CB, CMG, DSO, TD, PC, JP, DL (1868 – 1947) was a British soldier and politician. He was a Conservative Member of Parliament from 1900 to 1904 and a Liberal MP from 1904 to 1922 (for Ilkeston from 1910 to 1922) and from 1923 to 1924. He was Secretary of State for War from 1912 to 1914, and as General Jack Seely led what was most likely the last great cavalry charge in history at the head of a Canadian regiment in the Battle of Moreuil Wood in March 1918.

Seely was a great friend of Winston Churchill and the only Cabinet Minister to go to the front in 1914 and still be there at the War's end. He wrote a biography of his cavalry horse 'Warrior' in 1934 which has been seen as the inspiration for the very successful novel, play and film 'War Horse'.

Jack's grandson the former jockey and horseracing commentator Brough Scott has written a biography of the man and his remarkable horse, both of whom made it through the war to a long and happy retirement.

"GENEROUS EMPLOYERS

During the war the Manners Colliery Company are making a grant of 5s. per week to the wives or dependents of any of their employees serving with the colours, either with the regulars, Territorials, or Ambulance Corps. They are also allowing 1s. for every child under 14".

"EAGER TO FIGHT

Ready response from the National Reserve. In answer to Capt. H. Newton's appeal for 40 old service men to swell the ranks of "G" Company (Ilkeston and Long Eaton) of the Notts and Derbyshire Regiment, the members of the Ilkeston Branch of the National Reserve massed together on Saturday and dispatched over 30 of their number to the Territorial Headquarters at Derby. They were 'played' up to the station by their own band, which discoursed patriotic airs on the G.N. [Great Northern Railway, Heanor Road] Station platform while the men were waiting for their train. They received a hearty cheer as the train drew out".

"WITH THE TERRIERS (Ilkeston Pioneer, 21st August)

We have received a [...] letter from a member of "G" Company (Ilkeston and Long Eaton) of the 5th Battalion Notts. and Derby Regiment, who is with a detachment billeted in a Hertfordshire village [name censored at the time but actually Harpenden]. He says : Arrived here on Monday. Sorry I did not write before but I have had no time. We are worked too hard and too long. We are billeted on private houses and my chum and I have got a good crib. [Harpenden] is a jolly nice spot, and is a residential quarter for London businessmen. It is not a town, only a village, but is nearly as big as Ilkeston; wide roads and commons and trees everywhere. The death rate here is supposed to be the lowest in England. There are only a very few shops here and a very few amusements. [Harpenden] is absolutely in the hands of the military. There are thousands of troops. Every house has at least three; in some as many as seven or eight. One old soldier says it reminds him of the siege of Ladysmith. The village abounds with orderly rooms and cook-houses, and gun carriages and artillery are always passing through the streets. We are doing long route marches in full marching order, and we know it too. I am in good health and spirits, and getting hard as nails. The food we get is very good, tough of course, but very plentiful".

The Pioneer on 4th September contains a further appeal for more "Terriers" [Territorial Army soldiers] and reports that some of the Town Hall staff had volunteered, including Mr Cyril Duro from the Town Clerk's Department and Mr J.F. Wilson, "Mr Williamson's clerk in the education office". Also, "Ilkeston's crack cyclist" Mr A. Trussell and Mr G. Page the "well known Secretary of the local branch of the Church of England Mens' Society" had added their names to the list of prospective recruits.

Author's Note : See later in this book for Private Cyril Duro. A Rifleman A.L. Trussell was killed on 1st July 1916 while fighting with the Queen Victoria's Rifles at Gommecourt. It is not clear whether this is Ilkeston's 'crack cyclist'.

"IN THE DANGER ZONE

Private Edgar Heesom of "G" Company (Ilkeston) of the 5th Battalion of Sherwood Foresters (Territorials) son of Mr Alfred Heesom of Bath Street, has dropped upon a very comfortable billet in Harpenden, where the battalion is undergoing a thorough training. In the course of a letter [...] he said 'two fellows tried to murder a signalman here the other day, but were frightened off. Attempts have been made to poison the water supply, but so efficient is the guard that they have not been able to. A man has been looked for - and now found - who has been giving away poisoned cigarettes and pills. We seem to be in the danger zone'".

The Pioneer of 11th September reported that recruitment was now proceeding "pretty briskly" and had been transferred to the Territorial Drill Hall on Stanton Road, under supervision of Mr C. Wilmot and Colour Sergeant Aldred, with local G.P. Dr Tobin as examining medical officer. "By last week-end, the call to arms had been responded to at Derby by 6,000 stalwart men, and still there is no lack of recruits".

FORESTERS FROM INDIA

[Pioneer of 11th September] "Among the English [sic] troops used in convoy work in connection with the contingent of fighting men brought from India to the scene of conflict in France were the men of the 1st Battalion Sherwood Foresters, who had been previously

Janet Barlow

A group of 1/5 Sherwood Foresters assembled at Awsworth (probably on Park Hill) before marching off to war - August 1914. These men were all 'Territorial' (part-time) soldiers, with jobs in civvy street. Most were miners.

engaged in coast defence in Bombay. The flotilla of vessels was convoyed from India to Marseilles and to complete the voyage it took a month. The Foresters proceeded from Marseilles to Plymouth and are now encamped in the South of England near Salisbury. Among the Ilkeston men in the Battalion are Privates Knighton, Williamson, Smedley, Fletcher, Froggatt, Goddard and Glossop. Private Thomas Knighton, having secured a few days' leave, landed in Ilkeston on Monday afternoon. Owing to the heavy demands made by Kitchener's Army there was a shortage of clothing, and this combined with the fact the 1st Battalion had left India in a hurry resulted in Pte. Knighton, son of Mr Henry Knighton, having to make his journey home to Ilkeston in his Indian summer khaki.

In spite of his heavy overcoat he has been shivering this week, for underneath he has been dressed in a thin tunic, khaki shorts and puttees, with a pith helmet completing his airy 'rig out'. He has been three years and six months with the colours, two years of which have been served in India.

The 1st Battalion is now 1,500 strong, the odd hundreds being reservists who reported themselves at Plymouth. The Battalion is expecting to be called for duty at the Front."

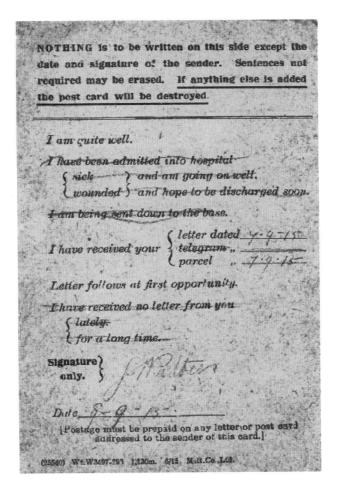

One of the official postcards used by troops in action.
No extra wording was allowed.

Grant Shaw

Richard Elliott was buried in the forest near Villers-Cotterets and now lies with his comrades in the small and moving 'Guards Grave' Cemetery

Megan Grace

The first casualty we know of from the district, Richard Elliott, in Grenadier Guards uniform during his pre-war service with the regiment.

Chapter Two

1914

The British Expeditionary Force - Mons - The Retreat - 'The Live Bait Squadron' - The Miracle of the Marne - Formation of the Trenches - HMS Bulwark

Richard Elliott
2nd Grenadier Guards, 4th September 1914

On 30th October the Ilkeston Pioneer newspaper rather flippantly said that 'the reported death of Private Richard Elliott (2nd Grenadier Guards) of Spencer Street, Smalley Common, is at least premature if not inaccurate' as 'although missing, his wife had noticed the words "dead letter office" on returned correspondence and had assumed it was he who was dead, not the letters'.

Sadly, Lily Elliott's feelings were indeed correct. Richard had been killed on 4th September as the 2nd Battalion the Grenadier Guards fought a vicious rear-guard action in the dense forest near Villers-Cotterets, south of Soissons in northern France. In the confused, close-quarter fighting that ensued, two platoons of No. 4 Company, were cut off and never received the order to retire. Under the command of Lieutenant the Hon. F.E. Needham and Lieut. the Hon. J.N. Manners, the two platoons fought on regardless. In the words of the regimental historian, "true to the traditions of the Regiment, they stuck to their posts, and fought on till all were killed or wounded". Lieut. Manners was killed. Richard Elliott is buried in the 'Guards Grave' Cemetery at Villers-Cotterets in the Aisne region along with ninety-eight of his comrades.

Born in Bulwell in 1884, Richard had worked as a coal miner/loader. He had married Lily Brown from Horsley Woodhouse in January 1911 and they lived with his widowed father John at 33 Spencer Street, Smalley Common. Unfortunately his service record has not survived, but evidence suggests he is the Richard Elliott, born in Nottingham who appears as a Grenadier Guardsman at Caterham Barracks, Surrey in the 1901 census. On completing his fixed term enlistment he would have been placed in reserve, which meant that Richard was 'mobilised' back into the army immediately war was declared in August 1914.

He was 30 years old when killed in action and is commemorated in the St. Andrew's Church Roll of Honour in Stanley. Richard is our first known casualty from Ilkeston and District, although as his death was not confirmed until the end of October he was not reported as such at the time.

George Irwin,
1st Irish Guards, 11th September 1914

George was born in Castleblayney, County Monaghan, Ireland in the summer of 1882. One of his first jobs was as a footman, but he enlisted in the Irish Guards in March 1903 aged 21. After

Jim was wounded in the war and brought back to Blighty to convalesce.
He is seen here (marked with a cross, next to crutches and only wearing
one boot) at hospital in Skegness.

Jim Beardsley (centre) and pals from the Sherwood Foresters,
with mascot, probably just before going off to war.

six years 'home service' he became a Police Officer in 1909, being stationed at Long Eaton and Church Gresley before moving to Ilkeston with his wife Agnes in March 1914. They lived at the 'Police Station' at 36 Bright Street, Ilkeston.

Although he had only recently recovered from a bout of pleurisy, George was one of the first reservists to be recalled on 4th August 1914, rejoining the Irish Guards at Wellington Barracks in London. The regiment were inspected by Colonel-in-chief Lord Roberts on 11th August.

George was appointed a sergeant with the 1st Battalion The Irish Guards, landing in France on 13th August 1914 and being sent to a concentration area some 40 miles south of the Belgian town of Mons. Taking part in the Battle of Mons and then in the long 'retirement' into France, the 1st Battalion the Irish Guards were in the thick of the action, losing over 100 casualties and their commanding officer until the 200-mile long retreat ended east of Paris on 5th September. On 8th September the Battle of the Marne commenced and the German advance was halted.

George died of wounds following an action at Vivieres, near Villers-Cotterets, about fifty miles north-east of Paris, probably on 11th September 1914. Although the Commonwealth War Graves Commission gives this date, his medal record states that he died two days later. The location of his grave was later lost, so he is remembered on the memorial at La-Ferte-Sous-Jouarre, east of Paris as well as on the Ilkeston Cenotaph and the Derbyshire Constabulary Roll of Honour. Although he only worked in the area for a short while before the war, George was generally regarded as 'the first Ilkeston casualty'. He was also the first Derbyshire Police Officer to be killed in the War.

George's widow Agnes was left to care for their two daughters, one year and four years old. His will named a policeman, Lewis Gurney, as his executor and he left an estate worth £166 16s 15d. After his death, Agnes and her infant daughters moved to Swadlincote.

Albert Edward Wheatley
HMS *Hogue*, "The action of 22nd September 1914"

Albert was born in Nottingham and joined the Royal Navy in 1900, serving twelve years. On leaving he was employed by the Stanton Ironworks Company and worked on the furnaces there. Being on the reserve, he was called up immediately at the start of the war and joined HMS *Hogue* at the Naval Base at Chatham. Although we have not been able to find very much more background on Albert, we do know that he survived this famous action in which three British cruisers were sunk in one day by the same German submarine.

HMS *Hogue* was a four-funnel cruiser built in 1900. 22nd September 1914 found her along with sister ships HMS *Aboukir* and HMS *Cressy* as part of a Cruiser Squadron patrolling in support of a force of destroyers and submarines based at Harwich which was intended to deter German warships from attacking the vital supply route between England and France in the eastern Channel.

Professional soldier
Thomas Edward Potter

'Ilkeston's first casualty'
Former PC George Irwin

Cyril Duro

William Henry Robinson

Though some concern had been raised about the vulnerability of these older cruisers (they had been nicknamed the 'Live Bait Squadron') their main danger was thought to come from German surface raiders and U-Boats were not regarded as a significant threat by the Royal Navy at this time.

At six o'clock in the morning on 22nd September, the weather was slowly calming after a storm which had caused some of the other ships in the squadron to leave and seek shelter in port. German U-Boat *U-9* surfaced nearby having waited out the storm submerged. She spotted the British ships and moved to attack. At 06:20, *U-9* fired one torpedo at *Aboukir*, the nearest ship. This struck her on the starboard side, flooding the engine room and causing her to stop immediately. No submarines had been sighted, so it was assumed *Aboukir* had hit a mine. The other two cruisers were ordered to close in and help.

After just under half an hour, *Aboukir* capsized, sinking five minutes later. *U-9* surfaced from her dive after firing the initial torpedo to see the two remaining British cruisers rescuing men from the sinking ship. Kapitanleutnant Otto Weddigen fired two more torpedoes at his next target, *Hogue*, from a range of 300 yards (270 metres). As the torpedoes left the submarine, her bows rose out of the water and she was spotted by *Hogue*, which opened fire before the submarine dived.

Both torpedoes struck the *Hogue*; within five minutes Captain Wilmot Nicholson had given the order to abandon ship, and shortly afterwards she capsized before sinking at 07:15. Five minutes later, *U-9* fired two torpedoes from her stern tubes at a range of a thousand yards (910 metres). One missed, so the submarine turned to face her one remaining bow torpedo toward *Cressy*, and fired at a range of 550 yards (500 metres). *Cressy* had already seen the submarine, had opened fire and attempted to ram, but failed.

Following the two torpedo hits, *Cressy* capsized to starboard and floated upside down until just before eight o'clock. Distress calls had been received by the rest of the squadron, which was already returning to the cruisers now the weather had improved slightly. Half an hour after *Cressy* sank, the Dutch steamship *Flora* arrived, having seen the sinkings and rescued 286 men. A second steamer picked up another 147. More were rescued by two Lowestoft sailing trawlers before the destroyers returned at 10:45. 837 men were rescued in total but 1,397 men and 62 officers, mostly part-time men from the Royal Naval Reserve had died.

One of *Aboukir*'s midshipmen, Kit Wykeham-Musgrave (1899–1989) survived being torpedoed on all three ships, being picked up by *Hogue* after *Aboukir* sank only to be torpedoed with her and then rescued by the equally ill fated *Cressy*.

Both local newspapers carried a report of Albert's ordeal. The Pioneer said that :

> "Leading Stoker Albert Edward Wheatley (RFR) a survivor of HMS *Hogue*, one of the three British Cruisers torpedoed in the North Sea last week by a German submarine, has reached his home at 51 Crompton Street, Hallam Fields, Ilkeston. The news of the great disaster in the North Sea last week came as a great shock to Wheatley's wife and family but their fears were dispelled when a few days later they found his name in the list of survivors. Their joy

was complete when on Monday night the husband and father returned to the cottage home near the great blast furnaces of the Stanton Ironworks Co. [...] [On the] fatal morning of the 22nd inst. he was then on duty in the interior of the great cruiser, in charge of seven other men, looking after the fires in No.7 stokehold. "I went on at four o'clock in the morning" said he [...] "and was on watch in number seven stokehold at seven o'clock when a torpedo hit us between numbers 7 and 8 stokeholds. I knew nothing about submarines being about. Immediately the stokehold was flooded, the water flooding in from the starboard side. I gave orders for the hands to get out up top, for I saw it was necessary to clear out at once. While we were going for the ladder I heard another bang. That meant a second torpedo.

The *Hogue* had heeled over to starboard after the first attack and now she was nearly gone altogether, and in five minutes was under water. When I got on deck she was heeling over terribly and it was a case of each man for himself. Throwing off everything except my flannel, I slid down the port side of the cruiser into the water. I swam away and got hold of a piece of wood that had been thrown over by order when the condition of the *Hogue* was found to be hopeless. Five or six other men got hold of the same means of support. The sea seemed covered with men. I could see the *Cressy* firing her guns. The sea was pretty rough and the water was pretty cold. I was rescued by the *Flores* [sic], a Dutch boat and landed at Ymuiden".

Wheatley could not speak too highly of the treatment given them by the Dutch. He spent two days in Holland and then came across on a Flushing boat to Sheerness. On the night of his arrival home a letter reached him that had been posted to his wife two days after the disaster, and on Tuesday morning there came a postcard that he had posted in Holland on the day his ship went down.

As he lay in bed, Wheatley wore a double thickness of clothing, his under flannel being the garment he wore when enduring the cold and fatigue of his terrible experience in the North Sea. Apart from his vain endeavours to keep warm and the involuntary quivering of his body he seemed fairly comfortable and content to be in his own home again."

John Harold Vann
King's (Liverpool) Regiment, 29th September 1914

John was born in Leicester, the son of James Wellesley Vann and Harriet Vann. His father was described as a 'hawker' and by 1911 John Harold was employed in a colliery at Clay Cross as an underground pony driver, a common job for the youngest workers down the pit.

He joined The King's (Liverpool) Regiment and was assigned to the 1st Battalion, "D" Company. Regrettably, his service record has not survived. In Aldershot when war was declared, they landed at Le Havre on 13th August 1914. By September he held the rank of Corporal.

John's regiment was involved in the battles in which the German advance was stopped just before Paris and then joined in several actions in the 'Race to the sea' which eventually ended in the formation of the trenches. It is not clear in which action he was wounded, but he died on

29th September 1914 'of wounds' near Versailles at the No 4 General Hospital. He is buried in Les Gonards Cemetery, Versailles, Paris. Corporal John Harold Vann was 21.

His widowed mother is stated to be of "Market Square Ilkeston" in the CWGC records.

William Henry Robinson
2nd Grenadier Guards, 5th October 1914

William was born in 1884 to John, a General Labourer born in Fulbeck, Lincolnshire and Maria. In 1901 they lived on Carr Street, Ilkeston and William worked in a colliery underground. 1911 found him working in Manners Colliery, now as a coal hewer and living in his brother's house, still on Carr Street. Aged 27, he is described as a widower.

The marriage and death records are not very clear but it may be that he is the William Henry Robinson who married Harriett Annie Grant in the winter of 1903 in the Basford District (which included Ilkeston) as a Harriett Annie Robinson died in June 1910. William subsequently remarried.

In any case, William had served some years in the army and remained on the reserve list so he was one of the first to be called up to serve with the 2nd Grenadier Guards. He was called out from work at the Manners Colliery when his mobilisation papers arrived. The Guards marched out of their barracks at Windsor on 12th August 1914 and following a train journey to Southampton landed at Le Havre after a poor crossing the next day. They were moved into Belgium (in cattle trucks) with the rest of the British Expeditionary Force and were welcomed enthusiastically by the local people. The retreat from Mons began shortly afterwards and the Guards fulfilled a covering role while the rest of the BEF fell back.

Sweating in the summer heat and carrying seventy pounds of equipment, they marched for an average of twenty miles a day for two hundred miles almost without rest until they had reached the River Marne north of Paris, where the allied armies halted and turned. On 6th September the French launched a counter attack which became known as 'the miracle of the Marne'. With the aid of six thousand French troops (moved to the front by six hundred Paris taxis) the allies fought a long battle until 9th September, the BEF suffering about 1,700 casualties. However, this move saved Paris and stopped the German advance.

The Germans had fallen back to the River Aisne where they had 'dug in' to await reinforcements. The BEF, equally exhausted, arrived at the Aisne by 14th September. By now the fine weather had ended and it had started to rain. On the thirteenth of September 2nd Coldstream had been at a place called Chavonne with the aim of crossing the Aisne. They had eventually crossed under intense German artillery fire which forced them to retire the way they had come losing three men killed and twenty two wounded during the process.

The following day the battalion had taken part in savage fighting for the heavily defended La Cour de Soupir Farm to the north of a village called Soupir. During this action they had suffered sixty six men killed or wounded. After this, the men of the battalion had assisted in

Victor William Wright (1897-1962) also survived the war. He is seen with sisters Beryl (left) and Gwen (right) and nephew Syd Cowley. His father was Joe Wright, the Barber from Ilkeston Market Place. His brother John Thomas Wright was gassed and died of bronchitis and heart failure aged 37 in 1925.

John Thomas 'Jack' Quinn joined the Leicestershire Regiment in April 1915. This shows him (left) with a friend whom his family believe was killed in action shortly afterwards. He became a PT Instructor in the Military Police and survived the war. He died in 1977 aged 81.

digging some of the first trenches of the war near the farm at Soupir. On 27th September Private Fredrick William Dobson had gained the battalion's first Victoria Cross since the Crimean War by rescuing a wounded comrade under fire.

While still in the trenches at Soupir, Corporal William Henry Robinson was killed in action on 5th October. He was 32 and left a wife and two children. He was quoted in the press at the time as 'the second Ilkeston casualty'.

He was buried in the churchyard at Chavonne but his grave was subsequently lost, so he is commemorated in a special memorial at the Bouilly Crossroads Military Cemetery just to the south-east of Reims in the Champagne area of northern France.

Thomas Edward Potter
1st Battn Sherwood Foresters Regt, 20th October 1914

Thomas was born in St Mary's Parish, Ilkeston in 1884, the son of James and Mary. His father was a coal miner.

By 1891 they were living at 11 Victoria Street, Cotmanhay. In 1901 at 16 years of age Thomas was working 'below ground' as a collier. The 1911 Census finds him as a professional soldier with the 1st Sherwoods stationed in India and now aged 26.

Called back from India, he landed in France on 8th September 1914. He was killed in action just a few weeks later on 20th October, aged 30. The location of his grave has been lost so he is commemorated on the magnificent Ploegsteert ('Plug Street') Memorial in Belgium.

His brother James Henry Potter was found to be medically unfit when he tried to enlist at the start of the war. He became a Special Constable instead but received at least one 'white feather' for not being in uniform. Brother Albert (q.v.) also died in the War.

Charles Arthur Roddis
Grenadier Guards, 6th November 1914

Private Roddis was another reservist who was called back to the colours at the start of the War and was described as being 'pretty much in the thick of it' since the Battle of Mons.

Charles was injured in the same action as Corporal William Henry Robinson and was invalided back to the huge Royal Victoria Hospital at Netley near Southampton, where he died a month later on 6th November 1914, aged 29.

His parents were Walter and Mary Ann Roddis and he had lived on Park Drive, Ilkeston and formerly in Cossall. Twelve of his relatives were stated to be serving in the army at his death.

The Ilkeston Pioneer newspaper said that he came from a 'famous fighting family'. In offering their condolences to Mr and Mrs Roddis, the Pioneer said that

> 'Sorrow stricken as he is, the father of the deceased soldier is proud to know that the vacancy in the ranks has been filled up by his younger son Frank, who has just joined the 5th (Reserve) Battalion of the Sherwood Foresters'.

Charles is buried in the Netley Military Cemetery in Hampshire.

Herbert Saunders Nunn
HMS *Bulwark*, 26th November 1914

Herbert was born in Ilkeston on 27th September 1880. His mother Catherine had died by the time of the 1891 census. His father William's occupation was stated as 'relieving officer'. He had three brothers, and there was a domestic servant living with them in 1891.

By March 1896, Herbert - aged 16 and described as a 'clerk' - had joined the Royal Navy as a 'Boy, second class'. That year he was sent to the school ship hulk HMS *Impregnable*, a wooden battleship built in 1860 and later to HMS *Ganges*, a wood-built former frigate now used as a training ship and moored near Falmouth.

He served on almost twenty ships and shore establishments in his career, being promoted through the ranks of Ordinary, Able and Leading Seaman to Petty Officer First Class by 1907. He seems to have seen service mainly in home waters except while on HMS *Crescent* (built 1892) when she was flagship of the Commander in Chief North America and West Indies Station. He also served in a fully-rigged 131 gun first-rate sailing battleship with a steam engine - HMS *Duke of Wellington*, built in 1852 and from 1907 to 1911 he served in the new (1905) armoured cruiser HMS *Warrior*, which later sank following the Battle of Jutland. He also served on the Admiralty yacht '*Enchantress*'.

In June 1913 he was posted to HMS *Bulwark*, a pre-dreadnought battleship launched in 1902 which in 1908 had been captained by Robert Falcon Scott, of Antarctic fame.

26th November 1914 found *Bulwark* moored at Sheerness in the estuary of the River Medway. In the early hours of the morning, her crew were in the process of loading coal and taking breakfast when a powerful internal explosion ripped the ship apart at 7:53am.

Debris from the explosion rained down over a distance of over four miles and caused damage to neighbouring ships including HMS *Formidable*, which would become the first Royal Navy Battleship to be sunk by a U-Boat less than two months later. The curtains from *Bulwark*'s Captain's cabin were found on *Formidable*'s deck and the explosion was heard as far away as Whitstable and Southend.

Out of *Bulwark*'s complement of 750, no officers and only 14 sailors survived, two of whom subsequently died of their injuries in hospital. Most of the survivors were seriously injured.

Herbert Saunders Nunn was one of those killed. In terms of loss of life, the incident remains the second most catastrophic accidental explosion in the history of the United Kingdom.

A naval Court of Enquiry established that it had been the practice to store ammunition for *Bulwark*'s guns in cross-passageways connecting her total of 11 magazines. The most likely cause of the disaster appears to have been overheating of cordite charges stored alongside a boiler room bulkhead, and this was the explanation accepted by the court of inquiry. It has also been suggested that damage caused to one of the shells stored in the battleship's cross-passageways may have weakened the fusing mechanism and caused the shell to become 'live'.
A blow to the shell, caused by it being dropped point down, could then have set off a chain reaction of explosions among the shells stored in *Bulwark*'s cross-passageways sufficient to detonate the ship's magazines.

Herbert was 34 years old and had been in the navy for more than 18 years. He is commemorated on the Naval War Memorial in Southsea, Hampshire. The Commonwealth War Graves Commission records his name as 'Herbert Sanders Nunn'.

Christmas 1914 at the Front

The Ilkeston Advertiser of 15th January 1915 carried extracts from a letter by Private C. Shelton of 16 Club Row, Ilkeston, which reminds us how good the postal service from home to the Western Front could be. He wrote to his family as follows:

"I think that I have received all of my Christmas parcels. I had one from Alice, and one from Helen, which I received on Christmas morning, and I enjoyed her pudding. I boiled it up in a billy can, and had it for dinner, and I enjoyed it and also the fags. Then I received another on Christmas morning from Bill Hodgkiss with milk, sugar, cocoa and bacca, and I set to and made a good tin of cocoa, for it was a fine frosty morning, and it warmed me up. I also received one from Aunt Lucy [...].

I often think of you and wish I was home again. You may think that I don't think nothing of any of you but I do, but don't get downhearted if no letters come, as I was on the trenches from the 11th December until the 2nd January. So you see we cannot get mails away, and we have had a very hard time of it this time. What with mudlarking etc., if you had seen us coming out you would not have known me, for we all were sludge from head to foot and wet up to the knees, for we have had a lot of rain this time in the trenches.

But we were all in high spirits, singing and joking with each other. I am glad that we are out now again for a rest, which we needed very much after our sojourn in the trenches for 22 long, weary days of rain and only two days' frost out of the lot, Christmas Day and Boxing Day [...] I am sending you my Princess Mary's gift home for you to take care of [...] Remember me to all inquiring friends."

Princess Mary's Gift

In 1914 Princess Mary's Christmas Gift Fund raised £100,000 to send every British soldier and sailor a tin like this containing comforts from home. This one was sent to Roy Naylor.
It also contained a Christmas Card and photograph of the Princess, the King's only daughter.

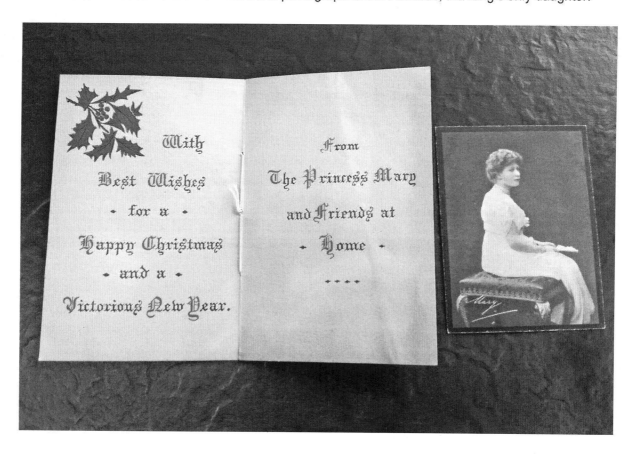

Chapter Three

1915

HMS Formidable torpedoed - 'Thrilling experiences at the Front' - Killed by shellfire -Hooge - Ypres - Tunnellers - Gallipoli - Brothers killed at Loos

William Durow
HMS *Formidable*, 1st January 1915

William, known as 'Billy', was born on 15th December 1896, the son of Joseph and Mary Ann Durow of West Hallam. In 1901 they were living at 33 The Village.

By the 1911 census they were living at New Street, Stanley along with his two year old sister and grandmother. Joseph and Mary Ann had lost three other children during their fifteen years of marriage. Joseph was a coal hewer but son Billy's occupation at 14 years old was as a saddler. At one time he was a choirboy in St Andrew's Church, Stanley.

Aged 17, he joined the Navy and was accepted with the rank of 'Boy, 2nd Class' on 20th March 1914. Billy's Naval record states that he was nearly five feet seven inches tall, had a 33 inch chest, brown hair and blue eyes with a 'pale complexion'. On 6th June 1914 he was posted to HMS *Formidable*. *Formidable* was a pre-Dreadnought battleship, commissioned in 1904 but due to the rapid pace of technological improvement she was almost obsolete by 1914. On his 18th birthday Billy was promoted to Ordinary Seaman.

On December 30th 1914 - just a couple of weeks after Billy's 18th birthday, HMS *Formidable* and a small squadron of battleships and destroyers set off from Sheerness in Kent on a voyage around the south coast to Portland in Dorset. After carrying out various exercises, the crews were disappointed not to be allowed ashore on New Year's Eve. The squadron exercised in line astern in stormy waters, with *Formidable* the last ship in the row. At 2.20am on 1st January in stormy seas as the squadron passed through some small fishing vessels, *Formidable* was seen to turn out of the line with a marked list to starboard. She began lowering boats. First thoughts were that the battleship had struck a mine, but it soon became clear that she had been torpedoed.

The torpedo had been fired by German submarine *U-24* at a distance of 360 metres. It had hit just level with the foremost of two funnels and had taken out one of the boilers, causing a loss of all steam power. The weather was worsening but two large boats full of men were launched. One capsized almost immediately after being struck by a wave. *Formidable* remained afloat however, so the U-Boat commander fired another torpedo from a distance of only 160 metres at 3.05am. This hit another boiler on the opposite side of the ship, which reduced the list and brought her back on to an even keel.

Debris from the explosion rained down on the boats and on the U-Boat, damaging its conning tower and periscope. The lack of steam power meant that some of the ship's boats could not be lowered, so the crew were ordered to break up decking and throw it into the water with anything else which could float. Despite the mountainous seas, one of the accompanying destroyers managed to pick up some men from one of the bigger boats, but *Formidable*'s Captain Loxley ordered it off to hail a passing liner. The liner did not respond.

The battleship remained afloat somehow, now in pitch blackness. The remaining crew, with little hope now of rescue, stood on deck smoking and singing until around 4.40am when *Formidable* gave a lurch and began to slip under the waves, bow first. Captain Loxley gave the order to abandon ship and many of the crew jumped in the water clad only in their 'fearnoughts', one-piece flannel nightwear.

The Captain was last seen lighting a cigarette on the forebridge, his faithful terrier 'Bruce' by his side. Men slid down the sides of the ship and most were not clear when she twisted to one side and slid under the waves. The rudder and screws stayed above the water for some time before disappearing into the dark sea. HMS *Formidable* thereby became the first Royal Navy battleship to be sunk by a German U-Boat.

Captain Loxley's body was never found, but that of 'Bruce' was washed up on the beach and given a proper burial. Although some of the men had been issued with 'safety collars' as a life preserver, these proved all but useless in the stormy seas. Some men were picked up by one of the destroyers, despite the wild waves. The rest of the squadron had already headed back to Portland.

Some of the men were rescued from the *Formidable*'s overloaded launch by the brave actions of the crew of a Brixham trawler, the *Provident*. The *Formidable*'s pinnace, a large boat originally containing 71 men, landed at Lyme Regis at 11pm the following night. Those aboard had had a heroic struggle, during which they followed a beam of light accidentally shown out to sea by the town's cinema projectionist, contrary to the blackout.

Some of the almost frozen men and bodies were thawed out in the Pilot Boat Inn, where the landlord's cross-bred collie took a keen interest in one of the men who was thought to be dead. Miraculously, he responded to her licking his face and the warmth of her body brought him back to consciousness. The dog's name was 'Lassie', and it is said by some that this is where the idea for the cinema's hero dog came from.

It is not known how the eighteen year old Billy Durow died, but his body was never identified, and he is commemorated on the Plymouth Naval Memorial. He is also commemorated by a plaque in the World War I Memorial Porch of St Andrew's Church in Stanley and on the Stanley Village War Memorial.

Author's note: Anyone wanting to learn more about the sinking of the *Formidable* and about its Captain Loxley, the career of *U-24* and its commander Kapitanleutnant Rudolph Schneider and the incredible stories of the survivors of the sinking should seek out the book "Before the Bells have faded" by Mark Potts and Tony Marks (ISBN 0-9528760-6-10, Naval & Military Press Limited, 2004).

Clarence Gordon Shaw
Lieutenant, 1st Lincolnshire Regiment

Known as Gordon, he was born in 1892 and lived on Stanton Road, Ilkeston. Although he joined the Sherwood Foresters, Gordon was given a command in the 1st Lincolnshire Regiment as Second Lieutenant in October 1914.

He featured on the front page of the Ilkeston Advertiser of 15th January 1915 under their 'Town Talk' header, describing 'His thrilling experiences at the Front' in the Ypres salient in Belgium.

"It was about the middle of October that he left this country for the seat of war. A message was received from the War Office to send someone to Grimsby to take out a draft of the 1st Lincolns [...] with whom he proceeded to France. On the way he lost eight of them - two falling out of the train - and saw nothing more of them. Five days after starting he was in the firing line at Ypres, and for 19 consecutive days and nights they occupied those trenches.

The men are not supposed to sleep at night as one never knows when the enemy may make a surprise attack in the dark; in the daytime however when the enemy's movements are visible, the men catch sleep in turns where possible. [...] Lieutenant Shaw described the trenches of his acquaintance as 'mud ditches' in which it became necessary to insert tubs inside on which men stood. At night the men got out of the trenches and repaired the damage of the day [...] One night one of the trenches contained about eight inches of water, and badly needing rest he got two ammunition boxes and placing them in the trench slept on them for about four hours.

At Wytschate [sic] some 10 to 15 miles south of Ypres, the 1st Lincolns lost 400 men on November 1st. There was a very nice spa here at that time, but on their return some time later it was a heap of ruins, the Huns being unable to resist the temptation to destroy anything that was beautiful. Lieut. Shaw saw whole villages being blown to pieces [...] In Ypres, the Cathedral and another fine building had been destroyed. The tower of the cathedral remained with portions of the walls with great gaping holes in them, while every window was blown away. He has seen the civilians fleeing from their homes which have been reduced to ruins by the Germans.

[...] Lieut. Shaw has had some stirring adventures and has been in some tight corners [...] Amongst the interesting incidentals of Lieut. Shaw's experiences was the capture of 60 of the enemy, amongst whom was an officer who was wearing the Iron Cross.

The noise of the firing of the guns and the bursting of the shells, which continues day by day, he describes as terrific and nerve shattering. Once they had about 30 yards of trenches blown in and they lost a lot of men. On the other hand he has witnessed the effect of our shells on the enemy's lines. A shell burst among the German trenches and arms and legs were blown into the air! One becomes so inured to such sights and to seeing men killed that little heed is paid to the fact, and there is no time for reflection. [...]

P.T. (Physical Training). One of these men is Samuel Bacon, whose grand-daughter Sheila Gillott sent us this photograph.

On four occasions a man next to him had been killed, two were struck by rifle fire and two by bursting shells. [...] Shells produce very funny and surprising effects. Some of the German shells, as we know, fail to explode, but here is an extraordinary incident witnessed by Lieut. Shaw. The day before he came away on leave a shell burst and the concussion lifted a man clean out of the trenches and dropped him on the ground at the back of the trenches, without harming him in any way! This man had not long been back from his recuperation after being wounded.

Christmas made a pleasant break in the monotony of warfare for many of the soldiers. Lieut. Shaw's company were relieved from the trenches on Christmas Eve by the Royal Irish Rifles, who very naturally were not a bit pleased at having to take their places.

The Lincolns went to a village about five miles away and were out of the trenches for four days. On Christmas Day they dined on roast beef and plum pudding and had plenty of tobacco and cigarettes to smoke afterwards.

Each soldier received a Christmas Card from the King and Queen, bearing the photos of their Majesties on one side and the autograph message on the other : "Our best wishes for Christmas 1914. May God protect you and bring you home safe. Mary R. George RI." Also a gilt box of choice design bearing a portrait of Princess Mary and the letter "M" on each side and around the border the names of the allies. The box contained a packet of cigarettes and a packet of tobacco, and with it was also presented a pipe. A Christmas Card also accompanied the gift and bore the greeting "With best wishes for a Happy Christmas and a Victorious New Year from the Princess Mary and friends at home".

Lieut. Shaw had a parting message to give. The Regulars at the front, he said, were 'fed up' and were badly in need of rest. They had been fighting continuously for months in the rain, and the muddy trenches, without any shelter, and it was time somebody went out to give them a much-needed rest.

He brought back with him a few interesting souvenirs of the war. One was the nose of a German shell [...] Another souvenir was a bullet from a shrapnel shell which struck a deal covering under which he sat and embedded itself in the timber. He cut it out with a knife and kept it. Had it come far enough its history might have been more tragic. A heavy service revolver he picked up in the trenches and this he retained. [...]

Lieut. Shaw looked remarkably fit and well and had a good healthy colour, while his face appeared a lot fuller than when he went to the Front. Campaigning has worked wonders for him, and with good fortune he will return with the inestimable satisfaction of feeling that he has done his duty nobly by loyally responding to the call of his King and country at a time when there is urgent need for the services of all young men sound in wind and limb."

The following week, the Advertiser printed a letter which Gordon had sent to his father on returning to the trenches.

"I arrived back quite safely, and joined my unit at 4am on the 12th. The biggest tragedy I've seen in this war so far was the departure of the boat train from Victoria. [...] There was the platform, crowded with men surrounded by mothers, wives, daughters and lovers. All were laughing and joking and chattering as if the men were off for a picnic. What a change when the train had started! Serious faces and eyes gazing meditatively into space. The scene on the platform after the train had gone I can imagine for myself although I didn't see it.

The last ten miles up to the trenches I had to walk. My thoughts can be better imagined than described. An empty, tree-lined road, not a soul to be seen nor a sound heard. Thoughts three hundred miles back in England, and dreams of home and beds and friends and firesides. Then suddenly a flash in the sky far in front reminded one of the guns again.

A few miles further I saw a star shell go up; further still came the boom, boom, boom of French artillery. Then at last I came within sound of rifle fire, nearer still a ricochette [sic] whirred past, and so with home fading into the background and war in its reality once more making itself the only consideration, I reached my battalion headquarters, reported my arrival, and proceeded to join my company in the trenches.

So - the end of leave and once more the struggle for the name and honour of the only country in the world worth living in or fighting for.

> Keep cheerful and remember
> God is a zealous pruner, for He knows
> Who, falsely tender, spares the knife,
> But spots the rose.

Ever your loving son, Gordon".

Gordon's efforts were recognised when he was 'mentioned in dispatches' and he was promoted to full Lieutenant.

He was one of the many local men killed on 1st July 1916 on the first day of the Battle of the Somme. Gordon was 24 years old and his body was never identified, so he is commemorated on the Thiepval Memorial to the Missing.

William Brown
171st Tunnelling Company, 20th April 1915

Unfortunately we have not been able to find out much background information on William; there are many William Browns and his service record seems not to have survived. All we do know is that he was born in Alfreton; we do not know anything about his personal life or age, nor do we know what his connection was with Ilkeston but it seems likely that he would have moved to work in one of the town's several collieries.

William originally joined the 11th Sherwood Foresters but he was transferred to the Royal Engineers where he used his knowledge as a miner to good effect as a member of one of the specialist tunnelling companies.

The 171st were known as 'the Kickers'. 'Clay kicking' was a form of manual digging using spades while lying down which was particularly effective in small spaces through heavy ground and would have been familiar to British miners.

Tunnelling was used as an effective weapon by both sides on the Western Front; although extremely dangerous for those doing the actual digging, a tunnel could be dug well under the enemy's lines and packed with explosives to be detonated at an appropriate time causing carnage and confusion which could then be exploited. It was a desperate business; the slightest noise might travel a surprising distance underground and could raise the alarm leading to a counter-mine being sunk by the enemy which could be detonated before your own, which would bury your own tunnellers alive. The enemy could also break through into your tunnel, leading to vicious hand to hand fighting in a very confined space. As a result, excavations had to be carried out in virtual silence.

William's unit worked for some time on a tunnel under German positions on 'Hill 60', used as an observation position at Zillebeke, south-east of Ypres. This tunnel was originally three by two feet in height and had been started by the French, but was extended when it became clear that Hill 60 was the only part of the German positions not waterlogged. When the battle of Neuve Chappelle started on 17th April 1915, this mine was blown with success; Hill 60 was captured with only seven casualties.

Three days later on 20th April, William was working on another tunnel when a German shell hit, and he was killed in action. He is buried in the Bedford House Cemetery, south of Ypres (now known by its Flemish name of Ieper).

Roland Hazell
2nd Sherwood Foresters, 29th April 1915

Roland was born in January 1884 near Amersham, Buckinghamshire to father John ('Jack') and mother Mary. At the time of his death, he had eight surviving brothers and sisters.

He married Lily Gomm on Christmas Day 1906 at the Parish Church in Amersham. On 11th May 1907 Lily gave birth to their first child, whom they named Elgey.

Roland joined the Oxfordshire Light Infantry some years before the war; his army record from this period has not survived. On leaving the army he would have automatically been appointed to the reserve.

He came to work at Cossall colliery and moved his family here after his army service ended. As a reservist, Roland was recalled to the army immediately war started. Leaving Lily with three young children and another on the way, he landed in France on 24th March 1915.

Roland Hazell was killed by shellfire while trying to save a child from a burning building.
Below : His widow Lily and four children; she holds little Lillie Le Bizet Hazell, who was born after her father's death. Lily herself died in 1919, leaving the children orphans.

This extract is taken from the 'Ilkeston Pioneer' newspaper of 21st May 1915.

"Rowland [sic] Hazell of 12 Grass Street, Ilkeston died the death of a hero while serving his country in France.

He was originally a full time soldier in the Oxfordshire Light Infantry, but left the Army and went to work at Cossall colliery. In 1914 aged 30, he re-enlisted and was transferred from the O.L.I to the 2nd Battalion Sherwood Foresters. He had only been in France for two months when he was killed by shellfire.

It appears the Germans were shelling a house which caught fire. Someone noticed an old lady by the building and she was successfully removed. She told the soldiers that a small child was still in an upstairs room of the house and Private Hazell gallantly went to recover the child. It was while he was on this noble mission that he was injured by shellfire. This was at three o'clock in the afternoon and Private Hazell never regained consciousness.

Writing to the sister of the deceased, who lived in Amersham Bucks, his commanding officer relayed the story of his gallantry, and expressed his deepest sympathy to his family.

Private Hazell was a tall, fine looking fellow, and the news has come as a terrible blow to his wife, who is keeping on the house in Grass Street. She is left with 3 little children, and is expecting soon to have an addition to the family."

Roland died from a shell wound to the chest. His body was originally buried in the graveyard to the convent at Le Bizet, on Belgium's southern border. After the war it was moved to the Strand Military Cemetery, just under a mile to the north near the Ploegsteert Memorial.

Just over two months after Roland's death, on 8th July 1915 Lily gave birth to a daughter whom she named Lillie Le Bizet Hazell.

Tragedy struck the family once more when Lily died suddenly of a brain haemorrhage on 15th July 1919; she was 36 and left four infant children. In 1922 the children were living with Rowland's mother in law, Sarah Farmer (who had been appointed their guardian) at Middleton Street, Ilkeston Junction.

Thomas Ernest Tillson
RMLI - HMS *Goliath*, 13th May 1915

Thomas was born on 25th August 1884 in Shirland. He joined the Royal Marine Light Infantry as a Private on 9th November 1901 at Worcester. His service record states that his religion was Wesleyan.

He was stationed mostly in home ports such as Deal and Plymouth and was promoted to Corporal in November 1904. However on 30th January 1906 while serving on the cruiser HMS *Argyll* he was reduced in rank back to Private - the cause of this reduction is not recorded. He

Grant Shaw

Berks Cemetery Extension, seen from within the
Ploegsteert Memorial, Southern Belgium

Dolores Watson

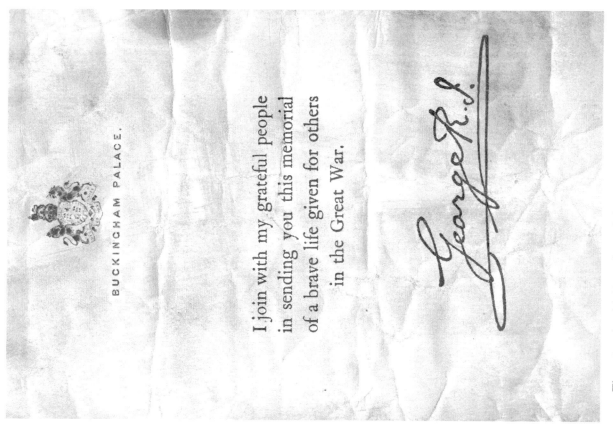

BUCKINGHAM PALACE.

I join with my grateful people
in sending you this memorial
of a brave life given for others
in the Great War.

George R.I.

The standard letter of condolence sent to the families of
all casualties on behalf of King George V

34

continued to serve at home and abroad at shore establishments and on cruisers HMS *Donegal* and HMS *Devonshire* and battleships HMS *Majestic* and HMS *Bulwark,* visiting Bermuda and Malta. He never regained his stripes, although his character was often recorded as 'very good'.

On 2nd August 1914 he was posted to HMS *Goliath,* a pre-dreadnought battleship which had been launched in 1898 and was mothballed until the outbreak of war. *Goliath* took part in operations against German East Africa, participating in the blockade of the German cruiser SMS *Konigsberg* in the Rufiji River, about a hundred miles south of Dar-es-Salaam in modern Tanzania.

From March 1915, *Goliath* was part of the ill-fated Dardanelles Campaign, and supported the landings at Gallipoli in April. On 25th April, she sustained some damage due to gunfire from the neighbouring Ottoman forts and shore batteries. She was damaged again on 2nd May. On 13th May 1913 while anchored off Cape Helles, *Goliath* was torpedoed twice by the Turkish torpedo boat destroyer *Muavenet-i-Milliye,* which was manned by a combined German and Turkish crew. After a massive explosion, the battleship capsized and was sinking when a third torpedo struck. She rolled over completely and sank with the loss of 570 of her 700 crew, including Private Thomas Ernest Tillson of the Royal Marine Light Infantry.

For sinking the *Goliath,* Turkish Captain Ahmet Saffet Bey was promoted to the rank of Major and Kapitanleutnant Rudolph Firle, the German Captain of the *Muavenet-i-Milliye* was awarded the Iron Cross First Class as well as other Turkish and Austro-Hungarian decorations.

Thomas Ernest Tillson was 29 years old. His body was never recovered and he is commemorated on the Plymouth Naval Memorial.

John Thomas Rigley
1/5th Sherwood Foresters, 14th May 1915

John was born in July 1880. His family lived on Queen Street in the following year's census and then on Graham Street for 1891.

He joined the army and served his full term in the 1st Leicester Regiment before being released and placed on the Army reserve. 1914 found him working as a collier with the Shipley Colliery Company, living with his wife Ruth, daughter Lillian (born 1908) and son John William (born 1909) at 6 Attenborough Row, Ilkeston.

John was called back to the army immediately war broke out and joined the local 'G' Company of the Notts and Derby Regiment (Sherwood Foresters). At 34 years of age, he was five feet eight inches tall according to his medical record. On September 3rd, while billeted in Harpenden, Hertfordshire, John - along with most of his comrades - signed an agreement to serve abroad if required. Territorials originally signed up for home defence only and could not be made to serve abroad without their consent; this changed when conscription was introduced in 1916. Reading between the lines, it seems that considerable moral pressure was brought on terriers to 'do the right thing' and volunteer, although very many were keen to do so anyway.

In January 1915 a new 'A' Company was formed under Major Marsden, to which John was attached. He set sail with 200 others from Southampton at 7pm, 28th February on the SS *Anglo-Canadian* and landed at Le Havre with the rest of the battalion the next day. The battalion War Diary states that while moving through France the troops were amused to have some rides on 'Old Bills', London buses which had been requisitioned for army use and still bore advertisements for the London theatres.

They took part in the Battle of Neuve Chappelle on 10th March but were attached to General Gough's 2nd Cavalry and saw no real action and no casualties were recorded.

However, John's luck ran out on 13th May when he was killed in a trench. The War Diary records that it was impossible to remove the body so it had to be left where it was. However, John's body was later recovered and buried in Kemmel Chateau Military Cemetery, South-East of Ieper (Ypres) not far from the border with France.

Ruth and the children were awarded a pension of 21 shillings a week; she also received John's personal effects contained in his holdall - razor strop, soap, shaving brush, razor, belt, matchbox, cigarette case, knife, two purses, spectacles, letters, photographs, cards and scissors. By May 1919 when she had to complete a list of dependants, Ruth had re-married to a man named Shaw and the children were living with John's sister Elizabeth Wright at Park Hill, Awsworth.

Roy Alan Eric Naylor
Royal Army Medical Corps, 15th May 1915

Roy was born in the summer of 1891 to Edwin and Elizabeth Naylor. In 1901 they lived at 153 Station Road; Edwin's profession was that of a colliery clerk. By 1911 the family were living at 15 Wilmot Street, and Roy was working as a Coal Miner (loader) underground. He had seven siblings, and the census says that his parents had lost three children, making eleven in total in 25 years of marriage.

He joined the Royal Army Medical Corps at the start of the war and arrived in France with the 22nd Field Ambulance unit on 7th October 1914. Unfortunately, his service record was one of those destroyed in the London Blitz but we do know that he was serving on the Western Front at Christmas 1914 when he received Princess Mary's Gift Box and the other items mentioned previously (see Clarence Gordon Shaw, above) which have been preserved by his family, and images of them appear in this book.

Roy and at least one of his comrades were killed on 16th May 1915 near Le Touret, about five miles north-east of Bethune. He is buried next to his friend, Harry Stapleton in the Le Touret Military Cemetery at Richebourg-L'Avoue. He was 23.

Roy's family carefully preserved many items relating to him and the various official notices which came after his death and most of these are reproduced in this book. They also saved his pressed asbestos identification tag.

Two months later, Harry Stapleton's mother wrote to Elizabeth Naylor from home in Tibshelf to clear up a suggestion that he had been buried next to his comrade Private Beardsley and her letter is also reproduced later in this book. She said "You have our deepest sympathy from a mother to a mother as nobody know what the awful blow is only them what as gone through it [sic]".

Roy's family have also preserved the letter from the Imperial War Graves Commission sending them details of the location of his grave and a photograph of it. That notice is also reproduced in this book.

John Waite
HMS *Triumph*, 25th May 1915

John joined the Royal Navy for a term of 12 years in June 1901. He was 19 years old and had been born near Lincoln, previously working as a carter.

During his 14 years in the Royal Navy, John progressed from 'Stoker Class 2' all the way to 'Stoker Petty Officer' in 1910. He served in a variety of ships and shore installations and travelled the world in ships such as the cruisers HMS *Minerva* and HMS *Blenheim* (a destroyer depot ship in the Mediterranean), transport ships such as HMS *Tyne* and the gunboats *Partridge* and *Woodcock* which patrolled the Yangtse River in China. Early in his career he also saw action in the South African (Boer) War. At some point he met Mary Jane Torr, who lived at 2a Coronation Street, Ilkeston and they married in late 1911.

On 2nd August 1914, while serving on HMS *Woodcock* in China, John was transferred at Hong Kong to the second class battleship HMS *Triumph* which had been stored in reserve but was now mobilized with a crew made up partly from the Yangtse gunboats.

Triumph had an interesting history, being built by Vickers at Barrow in Furness for the Chilean Navy as the *Libertad*, but purchased unfinished by the Royal Navy as *Triumph* before starting service in 1904.

Triumph was soon ready for sea and set off from Hong Kong on 6th August 1914, taking part in operations against the Imperial German Navy's East Asia Squadron (commanded by Admiral Graf von Spee) in early August, capturing a collier ship. On 23rd August she was attached to the Imperial Japanese Navy's Second Fleet and took part in the campaign against the German colony at Tsingtao (modern Qingdao) in north-east China, and helped capture it. With Tsingtao in Japanese hands, *Triumph* returned to Hong Kong for a refit in November.

Roy Naylor's family preserved many of his effects, including his pink pressed asbestos identity tag and the original notice regarding his burial. The image above shows Roy (second left) at camp, possibly in training and the image below shows Roy, second left and friends posing before the war.

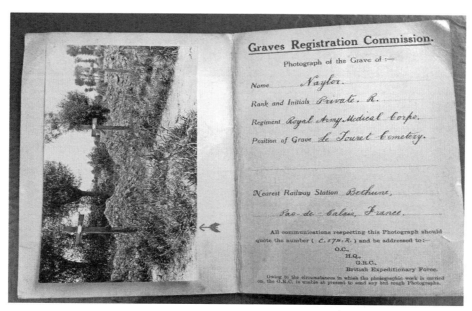

With the refit complete, *Triumph* was transferred to the Dardanelles. She left Hong Kong on 12th January 1915 and stopped at Suez from 7th to 12th February before moving on to join the Dardanelles Squadron. *Triumph* took part in the opening attack on the entrance forts on 18th and 19th February, and joined in the attack on the fort at Sedd-el-Bahr on 25th February. She, *Albion* and *Majestic* were the first Allied battleships to enter the Turkish Straits on 26th February. She also took part in the attack on Fort Dardanos on 2nd March 1915.

Triumph joined in the attack on the Narrows forts on 18th March and fired on enemy trenches at Achi Baba on 15th April. On 18th April, one of her boats torpedoed and sank the Royal Navy submarine *E15*, which had run aground and was in danger of being captured by the enemy. *Triumph* supported the main landing by the Anzacs at Gaba Tepe on 25th April, and continued to support them through May. On 25th May, the ship was underway off Gaba Tepe, firing on Ottoman positions with torpedo nets out and most watertight doors shut, when she sighted a periscope 300 to 400 yards (270 to 370 metres) off her starboard beam at about 12:30pm. This was the German submarine *U-21*.

Triumph opened fire but was almost immediately struck by a torpedo, which easily cut through the torpedo net on her starboard side. A tremendous explosion resulted, and *Triumph* started to list to starboard. The destroyer *Chelmer* evacuated most of her crew before she capsized ten minutes later.

She remained afloat upside down for about thirty minutes, then sank in about 180 feet (55 metres) of water. 78 of her crew died, including John Waite who was presumably at his post in the stokehold deep below the waterline. He was aged 33.

Cyril Duro
1/5th Sherwood Foresters, 26th June 1915

Cyril was born in 1896 to Joseph Baker Duro and Harriet Duro. His father was Inspector of Nuisances for Ilkeston Corporation for several years before (and after) the war and in 1911 Joseph and Harriet lived with their eight children at 113 Park Road Ilkeston. Cyril was at that time employed as a clerk in the Duke of Rutland's estate office on Lord Haddon Road.

On 4th September 1914 the Ilkeston Pioneer newspaper announced that among the volunteers for the local 1/5 Sherwood Foresters was Cyril Duro, 'of the Town Clerk's Department'.

Cyril landed in France on 1st March 1915. While serving in 'A' Company in the trenches, he was killed by enemy shellfire on 26th June and is buried in Sanctuary Wood Cemetery, near Ieper (Ypres), Belgium. Cyril is in fact the only Great War casualty named Duro in the Commonwealth War Graves Commission database.

His brother, Trooper 'Ted' (Edward Augustus) Duro was already on service with the Derbyshire Yeomanry when Cyril joined up, and according to the Pioneer of 4th September 1914 was proving useful to his regiment. Having been apprenticed to Mr J.E. Clarke's Wharncliffe Road Bakery, he was now "installed as regimental cook, and has found a special way of showing little favours towards his mates from Ilkeston, who keenly relish his cakes and pastries". Ted made it through the war and died in Southampton in 1956 aged 60.

Arthur Osborne
9th Bn., King's Royal Rifle Corps, 30th July 1915

Born on 2nd March 1895, in the 1901 census Arthur is living with his parents Lizzie and William at 45 Stratford Street, Cotmanhay. Ten years later the family are living at 9 Albert Villas, Station Road and the 17 year old Albert is a Pony Driver underground at a colliery. He lives in the same house with his parents, nine siblings and a boarder.

He joined the King's Royal Rifle Corps in February 1915 and was sent to their depot at Winchester for his training. Arthur's service record has a clean conduct sheet for his short time in the army. He arrived in France on 29th June 1915 and was posted to Hooge, east of Ypres in Belgium.

Arthur was killed at Hooge just one month later on 30th July.

To add to their grief, his family were not informed of his death until later. His service record contains a memorandum from father William dated 9th September saying he had had no news from Arthur since 20th July. The unhelpful reply was that Arthur seemed to have been given two regimental numbers on enlistment and asking for further details of his actual service number. It is not known when the family were actually notified of his death; it may be that Arthur's body was lost in ground which was not accessible until much later.

Arthur Osborne was aged 21. His body never was identified, so he is remembered on the Menin Gate Memorial at Ypres.

Frederick William Hazelgrove
Durham Light Infantry, 9th August 1915

Frederick was born in July 1884 at Little Eaton. He joined the Durham Light Infantry at Nottingham in 1903 when he was 18 years old, at which time he was stated to be five feet four inches tall with a fresh complexion, grey eyes and light brown hair, His religion was stated as 'Church of England' and he had been previously been working as a collier.

He served in the UK before arriving in India in December 1904. One year and 65 days later he was back serving at 'Home' until 21st February 1906 when he was released and transferred to the Army Reserve.

His service record shows that he suffered from eczema at the start of his service and was also treated for minor problems on a couple of other occasions. He was brought up on charges three times, once at the base in Newcastle, once at Aldershot and finally at Lucknow in India. Unfortunately the nature of these charges and the punishment given have fallen victim to the

6 Jessamine Terrace
Tilzhelf
Nr Alfreton
July 14/1915

Dear Mrs Naylor

I am taking the liberty in writing to you I am the Mother of Harry Stapleton who die with your son, Roy Naylor and I believe he was buried same time I had a Ilkeston Advertiser sent me by Mr Stapleton builder it said that your son & Private Beardsley die together and was buried in the same grave but I found out it was wrong as it is my son & your son as Mrs Beardsley wrote to me to say her son die in the Hospital on the Wendesday following and you have our deepest sympathy from a Mother to a Mother as nobody know what the awful blow is only them what is gone through it they is no letters now, none to answer and nothink to do for them now I see the same officer wrote to you what wrote to me I had a letter from a young fellow last Thursday & me from another young fellow Saturday morning to tell me were Harry was bury it is at La Touret Cemetry No 2, at Prue-do-Bois Cemetry, 5 miles about North Bethune perhaps you have heard I am sending you a m. ribbon of Harry I will send you a Photo of him when they are done. I would like one of your son if you have me I hope this will find you in good health as it leaves me.

From Your Truly Mrs Stapleton
6 Jessamine Terrace Tilzhelf Nr Alfreton Der

The letter which Roy Naylor's mother Elizabeth received from
the mother of one of his pals, killed at the same time.

water damage caused during the London Blitz, but it cannot have been anything too serious. He did not, though, rise above the rank of Private during his first period of service.

Frederick went to live at Trowell and attended Army Reserve Training in at least 1907 and 1909. On 1st August 1908 he married Emma Hawley at St Helen's Church, Trowell and they settled down at Trowell Forge. The 1911 census finds Frederick's widowed father Robert living with them. He is stated to be a stationary engine driver at a needle factory and Frederick is an Iron Pipe Fettler at a blast furnace. Fred and Emma had a daughter, Hilda, on 30th June 1912.

Being in the Reserve, Frederick was one of the first to be 'mobilised' at the beginning of August 1914 and reported to the Durham Light Infantry's base at Newcastle upon Tyne. He landed in France on 8th September 1914, and on 19th fought as part of the 6th Infantry Division at the Battle of the Aisne.

They were stationed around Armentieres for the winter and fought at the Battle of the Yser (which helped stop the Germans occupying the small part of Belgium left free after 1914) in April 1915. On 24th June Fred was appointed unpaid lance corporal - his only recorded promotion. July and August 1915 found the DLI at the Battle of Hooge, east of Ypres (Ieper) in Belgium. This was the first action in which the Germans had used flamethrowers and the 2nd DLI lost nearly 500 casualties, including on 9th August Frederick William Hazelgrove. He was 31 and his body was never identified, so he is remembered on the Menin Gate Memorial at Ieper.

At first posted as 'missing', Fred was not confirmed as having been killed in action until later - a letter from the Rector of Trowell (Rev. Nicholls) to the Army dated 29th August begs them to confirm whether Fred had died, as Emma had already heard this from his comrades. No reply has survived. It was not until March 1916 that Emma and Hilda were awarded a pension of fifteen shillings a week.

Frederick Bancroft
9th Sherwood Foresters, 9th August 1915

Fred Bancroft was born in West Hallam in March 1875. His parents were George and Mary. The 1891 census has them living in School Square, and Fred is a coal miner. On 18th July 1903 he married Kate Glenn from Ockbrook in the Parish Church at Dale Abbey at the age of 28. By the 1911 census they were living at 22 Lord Haddon Road, Ilkeston. They had no children.

At some time he served in the Sherwood Foresters before the war, and when his 'time expired' he was placed on the reserve list.

Fred was sworn back into the army on 14th August 1914 for 'one year or the duration of the War'. His service record - which has largely survived the WW2 blitz, unlike so many others - says that he was five feet six and a half inches tall with hazel eyes and brown hair. His religion is stated as 'Church of England'.

Posted to the 9th Battalion The Sherwood Foresters, Fred as an old soldier was promoted to Corporal just four days after rejoining the army, a rank which he retained throughout his service. On 18th October 1914 the 11th (Northern) Division, of which the 9th Sherwoods was part, were inspected by Lord Kitchener, Secretary for War, at Belton House near Grantham.

The Division was sent to support the campaign in the Dardanelles, Turkey against Germany's ally the Ottoman Empire and embarked ship at Liverpool on 30 June 1915, with much of the Division sailing on the requisitioned liners *Aquitania* and *Empress of Britain*. On 6th to 7th August 1915 the Division landed near Lala Baba at Suvla Bay and formed part of the new IX Corps.

IX Corps had the misfortune to be commanded by one of the least capable generals in the army, Lieutenant-General Sir Frederick Stopford. He had little experience of combat and although 61 years of age had never commanded men in battle. Stopford had actually retired in 1909 and got the job purely on his seniority to other more suitable generals.

The plan was for a new landing at Suvla Bay to relieve the troops already pinned down by previous action at 'Anzac Cove'. The objective of IX Corps was to seize the ring of hills that surrounded the Suvla plain. However, the orders issued by Stopford were imprecise, leaving room for interpretation. Their Ottoman enemy was led by a few German officers and eventually by a very capable, ruthless and decisive general Mustafa Kemal - who after the war was the main founder of the Republic of Turkey and is now better known as 'Ataturk' ('father Turk').

The landing started in chaos, in pitch darkness which led to confusion with units becoming mixed and officers unable to find where they were or to locate their objectives. Later, when the moon rose, they became targets for Ottoman snipers. Attempts to capture Hill 10 failed because no one in the field actually knew where Hill 10 was.

When the sun came up, Hill 10 was found and taken, the Ottoman rearguard having withdrawn during the night. General Stopford had chosen to command the landing from a sloop, HMS *Jonquil*, but while the landing was in progress he went to sleep, being woken up some hours later.

War correspondent Ellis Ashmead-Bartlett witnessed the landing after dawn. He could hear the fighting going on at Anzac Cove, but Suvla was comparatively quiet and "no firm hand appeared to control this mass of men suddenly dumped on an unknown shore." The Official History is to the point; "It was now broad daylight and the situation in Suvla Bay was verging on chaos."

No real progress was made on 7th August; the day was very hot and the soldiers became desperate for drinking water. IX Corps had suffered 1,700 casualties in the first 24 hours, which was more men than the total size of their Ottoman opposition.

Kemal was more than a match for Stopford and he held the high ground, content to remain on the defensive. The intensity of the fighting increased on 9th August but the opportunity to make a swift advance on the Ottomans had now disappeared. Around noon, gunfire set scrub alight

No. *Ro/338c*

(If replying, please quote
above No.)

R.A.M.C Record Office,

Aldershot Station.

21. 0 , 1915

SIR,

It is my painful duty to inform you that a report has this day been

received from the War Office notifying the death of (No.) *9767*

(Rank) *Pte* (Name) *Roy Taylor*

(Regiment) *R.A.M.C. No 22 Field Amb.* which occurred at

British Expeditionary Force on the *16th*

of *May 1915* , and I am to express to you

the sympathy and regret of the Army Council at your loss. The cause

of death was *Killed in action*

Any application you may wish to make regarding the late soldier's

effects should be addressed to "The Secretary, War Office, Whitehall,

London, S.W.," and marked on the outside, "Deceased Soldiers' Effects."

I am,

SIR,

Your obedient Servant,

J. Thomson
Colonel

Officer in charge of Records.

1354 5009 6—16 H W V   4 13 27

The letter which every family dreaded -
This is the official notification of death form.

44

on Scimitar Hill, and Ashmead-Bartlett, watching from the hill called Lala Baba, saw the British wounded trying to escape the flames:

"I watched the flames approaching and the crawling figures disappear amidst dense clouds of black smoke. When the fire passed on little mounds of scorched khaki alone marked the spot where another mismanaged soldier of the King had returned to mother earth."

Fred Bancroft may well have been one of these, as he was killed in action that day. He was 40 years old. His body was never identified, so he is commemorated on the Helles Memorial, some miles to the South right at the tip of the Gallipoli Peninsula.

Sydney Stuart Raines,
Derbyshire Yeomanry, 21st August 1915

Sydney was born in 1888 in the parish of St. Marylebone, London. The 1891 census has him living with his parents James (a domestic servant) and Mary at 244 Balcombe Street, Dorset Square, London. His parents had been born in Devon and Northamptonshire respectively and he had a younger brother, Reginald. By 1901 he and his now two brothers were living with their widowed mother at 23 Granby Street, Ilkeston. His mother was working for herself as a dressmaker. Sydney found a job at Manners Colliery and a love of horses, which he took with him into the army.

His army records have not survived, but we can tell from his medal record that Sydney joined the cavalry - the Derbyshire Yeomanry, which was first assigned to coastal protection duties in Norfolk. Later part of the Yeomanry was sent to aid in the Gallipoli campaign and Sydney landed in Egypt on 27th April 1915. On 21st August 1915 Sydney found himself, without his horse, taking part in the final attempt to connect the two landing grounds at Anzac Cove and Suvla Bay in the Gallipoli Peninsula in Turkey. His Second Mounted Division had been moved to Suvla as additional reinforcements and they took position on the far side of a salt lake near a hill called Lala Baba.

They joined in the second attack on 'Scimitar Hill', which was the largest attempted by the allies at Gallipoli. Marching in extended formation, they advanced straight across the salt lake and were under fire the whole way. For a second time the hill was briefly captured, before being lost for the final time.

This was the end for the Gallipoli campaign and by the close of the year all troops had evacuated.

Sydney Stuart Raines was killed in action on 21st August in the attack on Scimitar Hill. He is commemorated on the Helles Memorial at the tip of the Dardanelles Strait along with another 20,884 UK, Indian and Australian casualties with no identified grave.

Harold Nathan Beardsley, Northumberland Fusiliers, 26th September 1915
James Gething Beardsley, Durham Light Infantry, 27th September 1915

The story of the Beardsley brothers only came to light when the author was walking through Ilkeston's Park Cemetery and noticed the details on their parents' memorial, which reads :

"...also of their beloved sons who gave their lives at Loos, Private James Gething D.L.I. aged 21 years Died of Wounds Sep. 27th 1915 And Lnc. Cpl. Harold Nathan, N.F. aged 20 years Killed in Action Sep. 26th 1915, Their Duty Nobly Done"

The 1901 Census shows the Beardsley brothers living with their parents Arthur William and Maria at 14 Ash Street, Cotmanhay. Arthur was a lace maker. They are still there in 1911, and the census shows that in total their parents had 11 children, one having died. James is a lace maker and Harold a lace draughtsman.

James volunteered for the Seaforth Highlanders in September 1914 but was soon transferred to the Durham Light Infantry and although promoted to Corporal was reduced to Private in May 1915 for 'disobedience of orders'; no further information is given. He landed in France on 11th September 1915. On 26th September 1915 he was injured with gunshot wounds to his chest, hands and face, and he died of his wounds two days later. He is buried in Lillers Communal Cemetery.

Sadly, Harold's service record has not survived. We do know that he landed in France on 9th September 1915 and that he was killed in action on 27th September 1915. The CWGC state that he was 19, not 20. He is remembered on the Loos Memorial as his body was never identified.

Arthur John Trueman
2nd Sherwood Foresters, 14th October 1915

Arthur was born on 6th January 1896, the son of William Trueman a Colliery Deputy, and Elizabeth at 45 Awsworth Road, Ilkeston. Educated at Trinity Infants and Granby Boys Schools, he was later employed at both Oakwell and Manners Collieries in Ilkeston. Arthur was a choirboy and for four years daily server at Ilkeston's Holy Trinity Church.

He joined up on 2nd September 1914 and later became a Lance Corporal in the 2nd Battalion the Sherwood Foresters (Notts & Derby) Regiment. After training in Derby and Newcastle he landed in France on 27th January 1915. After two months he was sent back home to hospital in Oxford suffering from frostbite. He returned to France in August 1915 and was wounded on 12th October, dying of his wounds two days later. He was 19 years old.

Arthur is buried in the Lijssenthoek Military Cemetery, south west of Poperinge in Belgium. A beautifully decorated Memorial Scroll was made for Holy Trinity Church incorporating his photograph, which is reproduced in the colour section in the centre of this book.

Chapter Four

1916

Snipers - The Indian Army in Iraq - The Battle of Jutland - Gommecourt and The Battle of the Somme - Mesopotamia Campaign - 'Accidental death'? - Lost overboard

Samuel Straw
11th Sherwood Foresters, 28th February 1916

Sam was born on 29th June 1893. In 1901 he was living with parents Sarah Ann and Frederick at 2 Chaucer Street, Ilkeston. By 1911 Frederick had moved out and 18 year-old Sam was a coal miner / loader underground. He enlisted in September 1914, ultimately serving with 'A' Company, 11th Sherwood Foresters.

Not long after landing in France on 27th August 1915, Sam was promoted to Lance Corporal. His family believe he had been approached to train as a sniper as he was a good shot, but he declined. Sam was a regular writer to his family and many of his letters have survived. Some are printed later in this book.

On February 21st, 1916 Sam was shot, probably by a sniper. The bullet entered his neck and did serious damage to his spine, resulting in him becoming paralysed. He was sent to the 4th General Hospital in Camiers, from where the Hospital Chaplain wrote to his fiancée (whom we know only as 'Miss Smith') on 26th February telling her of the seriousness of his wounds.

Two days later Sam died, aged 23. He is buried in Etaples Military Cemetery, Pas de Calais, France.

George Henry Tinkler
2nd Leicestershire Regiment, 1st March 1916

Born in Ilkeston in January 1897, in the 1901 census 4 year-old George and his parents Samuel (an Ostler/groom) and Louisa were living at 3 Wilmot Street. He was their first child. Ten years later and George has a seven year old sister and baby brother. Now they are living at 16 Fullwood Street and both father and son work at a colliery, Samuel continuing his care of horses as a 'Colliery Horse Keeper (Underground)'. George too is a pony driver, aged 14 although he does not work underground.

We know that George joined the 2nd Leicesters, which were attached to the 7th (Meerut) Division of the British Indian Army Expeditionary Force and had been fighting on the Western Front since not long after the war began. The division consisted mostly of Indian-born troops. They eventually left the trenches in November 1915 and arrived in Mesopotamia early the following year, participating in the battles at the Sheikh Sa'ad, Wadi and Hanna in modern Iraq which led a year later to the capture of Baghdad.

Above : Samuel Straw looking casual, without his uniform jacket or cap.
Below : Sam Straw (second from right) and friends. Sam said that this photograph
'was alright' but made him 'look sleepy'. Sam died on 28th February 1916 aged 23.

Both : Margaret Richardson

48

However, George Henry Tinkler was seriously injured and died of his wounds not long before the Battle of Dujailia on the banks of the River Tigris on 1st March 1916. He was aged just 19.

George's regiment fought in an Indian Division and some official records state that he died in India. This is probably incorrect but in any case we do know that the location of his body was lost.

He is commemorated on the Kirkee Memorial at Khadki near Pune (Poona), about 90 miles south east of what he would have called Bombay but we now know as Mumbai.

Francis George Swann Walters
7th King's Royal Rifle Corps, 13th March 1916

Frank, as he was known, was born in the Summer of 1896. His parents lived at 54 Lord Haddon Road. His father Joseph Middleton Walters was a School Master and by 1911 is described in the census as "Head Schoolmaster". We know that he was Headmaster of the Chaucer Junior School and at this time he and wife Harriett lived at 33 Drummond Road with their only child Frank and a servant girl Annie Lee who was aged only 14.

Frank joined the King's Royal Rifle Corps in Nottingham with the rank of Rifleman. He landed in France on 3rd August 1915.

Sadly his service record has not survived, but we do know that Frank was killed in action on 13th March 1916, aged just 19. He is buried at the Cabaret-Rouge British Cemetery at Souchez, on the opposite side of the Autoroute from the massive Vimy Ridge Memorial in the Pas-de-Calais, Northern France.

John Mottram,
1st Leicestershire Regt., 24th March 1916

John was born in around 1892 in either Watnall or Kimberley. In 1901 he was living with parents Harriett Ann and Abraham in Kimberley, and in the summer of 1910 he married Mary Ann Meakin.

By the 1911 census they were living on High Street at Kimberley and Mary's widowed mother Sarah was visiting. John was a loader at a colliery. Mary Ann and John had at least two sons, Arthur (born early 1913) and Albert E. (born Summer 1914). They later lived in Cotmanhay at 3 Hallsworth Yard.

John enlisted in the 1st Battalion the Leicestershire Regiment and arrived in France on 5th December 1915. He died in a field hospital of severe shrapnel wounds just over three months later on 24th March 1916, aged 24. He is buried in the huge Etaples Military Cemetery (the largest CWGC cemetery in France) not far from Boulogne.

Above : Alban Eaton
Left : James Walters, wife Gertrude and son George taken while on leave in August 1915.

Below : James Walters while convalescing after his scalp wound (he is the one with a bandaged head, centre).

In John's possessions was a card bearing the following poem :

"God bless my Daddy, who's away across the silver sea,
Fighting in the cause of right for home, and Mum, and me,
Please God take care of Daddy dear through sunshine and through rain,
And wipe away poor Mummy's tear and send him home to me"

James Walters
1st Sherwood Foresters, 29th May 1916

James was born in June 1886 to George and Maria of Attenborough Row, Norman Street, Cotmanhay.

He joined the army in 1904, aged just 17. His service record has survived, and this shows he exaggerated his age by about a year. His medical record shows us that he had trouble with his teeth at the time he enlisted. Serving at home, army life must have suited him as on 13th October 1906 he extended his contract to serve in the army to a full seven years, and he arrived in India on 19th December 1906.

It was four years and 39 days until he was posted back home again. His medical record says he was treated for 'enteric fever' on 17th June 1907.

James obtained a certificate of education from the army in 1908 and a qualification enabling him to join the mounted infantry while in India. His term in the army over, he arrived back in the UK on 26th January 1911 and was transferred to the Army Reserve on 28th January. He found work locally as a miner and the 1911 census found him boarding along with his brother John Thomas Walters with the Dawes family at 41 Albert Street, Ilkeston.

He married Gertrude Kershaw on 14th December 1912 at the Register Office at Basford. Their son George was born on 12th July 1914.

James was mobilised at Derby on 7th October 1914 and left for France, landing at Le Havre on 4th November 1914.

On 18th January 1915 he received a gunshot wound to the scalp, spent some time in hospital and was sent to a convalescent hospital in February. A photograph has survived of him in his hospital uniform (blue uniform with white shirt and red tie) with some hospital staff and other patients, which is printed in this book. On 27th February he was sent back to light duties at the regimental depot at Honfleur before rejoining his unit on 10th March. James was immediately promoted to Lance Corporal and once more to Corporal in August.

On 21st to 27th August 1915 he was allowed leave and hastened home to have his photograph taken with Gertrude and baby George - this has survived and is printed in this book. In September James sent Gertrude two of the 'pro forma' service postcards which allowed only a limited amount of information to be given by front line troops - these too have survived.

A Memorial Card printed by the family of James Walters and his headstone
in the Fosse No.10 Communal Cemetery Extension, Sains-En-Gohelle in the far north of France,
not far from the Belgian border.

Anne Cook

Grant Shaw

Often we pause and think of you,
And think of how you died;
To think you could not say "goodbye"
Before you closed your eyes.

No loved one stood beside you
To hear your last farewell,
Not a word of comfort could you have
From those who loved you well.

In Loving Memory

of

Corporal James Walters

(1st SHERWOOD FORESTERS).

the dearly beloved husband of
Gertrude Walters.

————

Who was killed in action,
May 29th, 1916.

————

Aged 29 years.

On 29th May 1916, James was seriously injured and he died of his wounds later the same day. He was 29 and his body was buried at the Fosse No.10 Communal Cemetery Extension, Sains-En-Gohelle in the far north of France, not far from the old Loos battlefield.

Gertrude and George were granted a pension of fifteen shillings and sixpence a week.

Frederick James Wicks
HMS *Queen Mary*, 31 May 1916

Frederick James Wicks was probably born on 19th September 1892 in Ilkeston. Some records give his date of birth as 17th September 1893. His parents were William and Bina. William was a farmer, and by the 1911 census the family were living at The Blob Farm, Awsworth.

Frederick James was a loader in a coal mine and is down just as 'James' on the census, so this may have been the name the family used for him (the 1911 census was the first one where the head of the household filled in the entries personally rather than dictating them to an enumerator).

He joined the Navy on 7th December 1911 for a fixed period of five years which would have been followed by an agreed nine years on the reserve list. His service record says that he was five feet three and a half inches tall, with light brown hair, hazel eyes and a fresh complexion. More colour is added by the note of his tattoos; he had a 'Japanese lady', 'true love' and an eagle on his right forearm and a lady, another Japanese lady, a soldier and a butterfly on his left. This information was recorded on Royal Navy service records for the grim purpose of identifying bodies lost at sea.

Rated 'Stoker, second class', he was posted to the ex-battleship HMS *Renown*, which was used as a stoker's training ship. He was posted to HMS *Minerva* in August 1912 and would have been present when *Minerva* took part in the rescue attempt when the submarine HMS *B-2* sank after a collision in October 1912. He was promoted to 'Stoker, first class' in December.

However, Frederick James seems to have transgressed in some way as he was given 20 days detention in May the following year (unfortunately the clerk's handwriting giving three words of explanation is illegible). However, he kept his rank and in September was posted to the brand new battlecruiser HMS *Queen Mary* on her commissioning day.

Just after the start of hostilities *Queen Mary* took part in the Battle of Heligoland Bight, in which a Royal Navy force lured several German warships into a trap, a plan approved personally by First Lord of the Admiralty Winston Churchill. The battle was a British victory. Germany lost three light cruisers and a destroyer; another three light cruisers were damaged. German casualties were 1,242 with 712 men killed including a Rear Admiral and 336 men taken as prisoners of war. The Royal Navy lost no ships and only 35 men killed, with 40 wounded. *Queen Mary* went through a refit in January and February of 1915.

Jutland 1916

The only major clash of fleets at sea of the war, it ended in confusion leading both sides to claim victory. The Germans had won in terms of ships destroyed, but the continuing threat from the Royal Navy meant they would never dare leave their bases again.

Above : HMS *Black Prince*, a cruiser launched in 1904. She lost contact with the rest of the fleet and was lost with all hands shortly after engaging the enemy forces. Among the dead was William Stokes, a 22 year old stoker who had lived on Carr Street, Ilkeston.

HMS *Queen Mary*, a modern battlecruiser. She was hit twice by the German battlecruiser SMS *Derfflinger* during the early part of the battle of Jutland and her magazines exploded soon afterwards, sinking her and killing Ilkeston's Frederick Wicks.

On 31 May 1916 *Queen Mary* put to sea with the rest of the battlecruiser Fleet to intercept a sortie by the German High Seas Fleet into the North Sea. The British were able to decode the German radio messages and left their bases before the Germans put to sea. The Germans opened fire first at 15:48; their fire was accurate from the beginning but the British overestimated the range, as the German ships blended into the haze. *Queen Mary* opened fire at about 15:50 on SMS *Seydlitz*, using only her forward turrets. By 15:54 the range was down to 12,900 yards (11,800 metres), and *Queen Mary* made two hits on *Seydlitz* in the next three or four minutes, one of which caused a propellant fire that burnt out one of her aft turrets.

SMS *Derfflinger* then engaged *Queen Mary* at 16:16. *Queen Mary* hit *Seydlitz* again just a minute later and knocked out another gun. In return, *Queen Mary* was hit three times by *Seydlitz*. By 16:25 the range was down to 14,400 yards (13,200 metres), and Admiral Beatty turned to starboard to open the range again. This move came too late, however, for *Queen Mary*, as *Derfflinger* hit her twice before 16:26. One shell hit the forward part of the ship and detonated one or both of the forward magazines, causing a massive explosion which broke the front third of the ship away. A further explosion, possibly from shells breaking loose, shook the aft end of the ship as it began to roll over and sink. The battlecruiser behind her, HMS *Tiger*, was showered with debris from the explosion and forced to steer to port to avoid her remains. Only eighteen survivors were picked up by the British destroyers, and two by the Germans.

Hopefully Frederick James Wicks, as a stoker deep inside the ship, would not have known much about it as the huge explosions ripped the ship in two. He was 23 and as his body was never recovered, he is remembered on the Portsmouth Naval Memorial. HMS *Queen Mary* has now been declared a protected place under the Protection of Military Remains Act 1986 to discourage looting and damage to the resting place of 1,266 officers and men. She lies in three pieces on the sea bed.

Joseph Eaton
1/5 Sherwood Foresters, 1st July 1916

Joseph was born in 1895 in Ashover. His mother died when he was very young and his father, also Joseph, does not appear in any records relating to his son until after Joe Junior's death. For whatever reason, our Joseph was living with his grandmother Mary Hopkinson, uncle, aunt and two cousins in Ashover at the time of the 1901 census, aged six years.

The 1911 census finds him as a 'visitor' in the household of John Mather and family at Hallam Fields. He worked for Stanton Ironworks in the pipe pits as an iron pipe moulder, although the census describes him as a 'general labourer'. He later lodged at 28 Stanton Road. Joseph joined the 1/5th Sherwood Foresters as a territorial (part time) soldier at Ilkeston on 11th November 1912, aged seventeen and ten months. The 'Territorial Force' was created in 1908 as a result of a reorganisation of the old Militia and other units. They were recruited locally by county, trained at weekends or in the evenings and went away to an annual Summer Camp. A man could join the territorials at 17 whereas (at least on paper) he would have to be 18 to join the regular army.

His record tells us that Joseph attended the annual camp in 1913. When war was declared, Joseph was one of those 'terriers' who had been at the 1914 annual camp in East Yorkshire and who marched away after a civic send-off from the town in August. He remained with the 1/5th through training in Hertfordshire and landed at Le Havre on 27th February 1915.

On 1st June 1915 Joseph was taken to a Field Ambulance Station suffering from a gunshot wound to the head. However this cannot have been too serious as he was sent back to his unit from hospital five days later.

Joseph's medical records give only a little information but the next entry says that on 12th November he was sent to the Field Ambulance, the reason stated being 'mental'. He was admitted to hospital and discharged two days later. However, the next day he was sent back to the base hospital in Rouen. Released from Rouen back to the base depot on 24th November, he was admitted again on 1st December. On 11th December he was sent back to rejoin his unit 'in the field'. There is no further information as to Joseph's condition during this period and we can only speculate what the problem was and whether it was connected to his being shot in the head six months earlier. There is no sign of any recurrence of this condition in his medical records.

On 1st July 1916, Joseph went 'over the top' in the attack on Gommecourt and was killed along with so many other local lads. However, his body was never identified and his record shows the agony his family must have been through not knowing if he was a prisoner, wounded or dead. He remained on the books as 'missing' until 25th August, when he was 'struck off strength', in other words it was acknowledged that he was unable to rejoin his unit. It was not until 13th January 1917 that the army officially stated that he had been killed in action. The Ilkeston Pioneer reported on 16th March 1917 that Joseph :

"was brought up (having lost his mother early in life) by Mrs Matthews [his] [...] aunt. His grand-mother, Mrs Mary Hopkinson, also lived with Mrs Matthews and up to receipt of the official notice clung tenaciously to the idea that her grandson was still alive. She was 85 years of age, and after all hope had been dissipated by the news of her grandson's death, she gradually sank, and was buried on Saturday last, having died the previous Tuesday. Private Eaton was 21 years of age".

Joseph's absent father was judged to be his next of kin and Joseph's effects were sent to him at Lower Birchwood, near Alfreton. Joe is remembered on the Thiepval Memorial, as his body was never identified.

Caleb John Stubbs
1/5 Sherwood Foresters, 1st July 1916

Born in Ockbrook, Caleb was baptised on 26th August 1894. In 1901 he, his parents John and Alice and his three younger siblings were living at Osmaston, near Ashbourne. His father was a coker in a gas works.

It has not been possible to trace the family using the online 1911 census; this might be due to transcription errors.

Caleb joined the Sherwood Foresters in Derby on 17th March 1915 and at that time he was living at 107 Kingsway, Ilkeston. He was five feet six and a half inches and when examined was found to be fit. His occupation was stated as 'pipe maker'. On the same day, he signed the agreement to serve abroad if necessary. Presumably while on leave, Caleb married Florence Tatham in the summer of 1915 somewhere in the Basford district (which included Ilkeston).

On 12th October he was transferred to the 1/5 Sherwood Foresters and landed in France the next day. He joined his unit just after the main action in the Battle of Loos on 18th October. On 26th October a representative party from the battalion was inspected by King George V near Bethune. Shortly after this the King was thrown from his horse and seriously injured. It was also around this time that the battalion received its first 'tin hats' - before this they had no head protection at all.

On 3rd May 1916 Caleb was appointed unpaid Lance Corporal.

Lance Corporal Caleb John Stubbs was another of many local lads who went 'over the top' at Foncquevillers, attacking the German positions at Gommecourt at 7.30am on 1st July 1916. He was killed that day, and is buried in the Foncquevillers Military Cemetery along with at least four other Ilkeston men. Caleb was 20 years old.

Florrie was awarded a pension of ten shillings a week, paid from January 1917. The parcel containing Caleb's effects was wrongly addressed and Florrie suspected that some items had 'gone missing' in transit. However, there is no evidence that anything else ever arrived.

Henry Shaw,
1/5 Sherwood Foresters, 1st July 1916

Henry was born on Bonfire Night, 5th November 1894. His parents were Arthur, a coal hewer and Annie Maria, nee Bostock. He was their first child, but brother Cecil Randolph, sister Nora Annie and little brother Samuel Edward arrived at two yearly intervals. Sadly, Sam died while still an infant. By 1911 the family were living at 139 Station Road, Ilkeston and both Henry and his younger brother Cecil were pony drivers 'down the pit'. Henry worked at West Hallam Colliery, behind High Lane Central but it is not clear whether the two brothers worked together. Henry joined the Church Lads' Brigade and his cap badge bearing the motto 'Fight the Good Fight' has survived.

Henry enlisted at Ilkeston as a territorial soldier on 20th May 1914, well before war broke out, aged 19 years and 7 months. He may have been one of the honour guard for the King and Queen's visit to Ilkeston in June 1914 and was most likely at the training camp at Hunmanby near Filey when the order for mobilisation was received.

William Hiorns of Park Road is buried at Wimereux on the coast near Calais, just a few feet from Lt. Col. John McCrae, the Canadian Doctor who wrote the famous poem 'In Flanders Fields'.

The CWGC plot inside the huge Calais Southern Cemetery in which Ilkeston's J. Tunnicliffe and Cotmanhay's John Hallam are buried

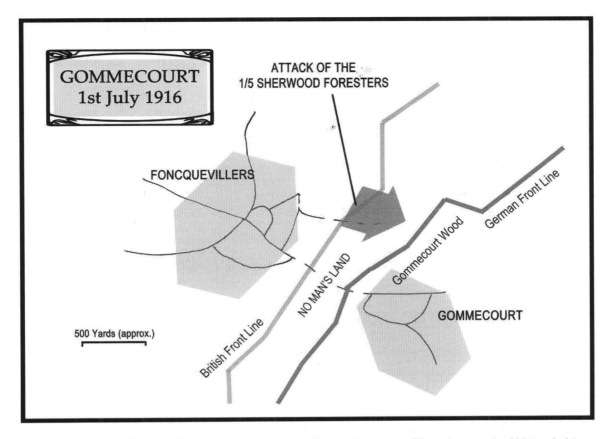

GOMMECOURT
1st July 1916

ATTACK OF THE
1/5 SHERWOOD FORESTERS

FONCQUEVILLERS

German Front Line

Gommecourt Wood

NO MAN'S LAND

British Front Line

GOMMECOURT

500 Yards (approx.)

Above : The 46th North Midland Division were one of two ordered on a 'diversionary attack' intended to take Gommecourt north of the Somme battle on 1st July 1916. Many Ilkeston soldiers were among them.
Below : The view today from the position of the British trenches from which Ilkeston's soldiers in 1/5 Sherwood Foresters went 'over the top' from 7.30am on a beautiful early Summer morning.

Gommecourt Wood

Both : Grant Shaw

59

He served as a private and was billeted in Harpenden, Hertfordshire with the regiment through the end of 1914 and into the beginning of 1915. While at Harpenden he volunteered for service overseas, signing his agreement for foreign service on 4th September 1914. Henry embarked from Southampton with most of the rest of the local 5th Sherwoods on 25th February 1915 for Le Havre.

Henry sent several letters to the local newspapers, some of which are reprinted later in this book. He survived the Battle of Loos in northern France in 1915 and in November of that year was promoted to unpaid Lance Corporal, this being converted to a paid rank on 7th February 1916 and to full corporal on 1st March 'in the field'. He was allowed only one short period of leave in this time, from 17th to 19th December 1915. It is not known whether he came home; presumably not due to the distance involved.

In February 1916 the 1/5 received their first two Lewis machine guns, more portable than the standard Vickers model and Henry received training as a Lewis Gunner. On 18th May 1916 he was promoted to unpaid Lance Sergeant and on 3rd June to paid Lance Sergeant. Some records and indeed his headstone record his rank as full sergeant although this is not reflected in his service record.

At 7.30am on Saturday 1st July 1916 Henry went 'over the top' with the rest of his company and his Lewis machine gun. We do not know exactly what happened to him; many were killed or injured immediately - the Germans were only a few hundred yards away in Gommecourt Wood - though a few made it to the enemy trenches. None of these are known to have come back.

Henry's friends told his parents that he had died instantly and that they had seen him buried with proper ceremony and dignity. The reality may have been quite different. Henry is buried in a part of the cemetery where the dead are interred so closely together there are three names on each headstone. This may indicate that it took so long before the bodies could be recovered that there was little left. Henry's will in his paybook (which he would have kept on him at all times) did not survive, which would add weight to that theory. In any case he shares a headstone with two of his comrades from the 1st/5th Sherwood Foresters in the Foncquevillers Military Cemetery, just a few hundred yards from where he died.

One of those with whom Henry was billeted in Harpenden in 1914/15 was Mrs Katherine J. Hutchinson of 2 Spencer Road Harpenden, and Mrs Hutchinson sent a moving letter of condolence to his parents after he was killed and which is reprinted later.

Annie Maria Shaw, Henry's mother took the opportunity to have a personal motto carved on Henry's headstone, which looks back to his membership of the Church Lads' Brigade. It reads "My darling boy. Fought the good fight and has been rewarded in Heaven. Love Mother". It is believed that she visited Henry's grave in around 1930 after the cemeteries were properly laid out by the (then) Imperial War Graves Commission. This was quite an undertaking at the time, but a surprising number of mothers and widows made the trip to France or Belgium on organised 'pilgrimages' in the 1920's and 1930's.

Henry Shaw was a miner from Ilkeston who joined the local 1/5 Sherwood Foresters as a part-time soldier before the War. Two years later and now a Sergeant, he was killed with many other local men during the ill-fated 'diversionary' attack on Gommecourt on the first day of the Battle of the Somme, Saturday 1st July 1916. He was 21.

Grant Shaw

Henry (left) shares a headstone with two comrades in the Foncquevillers Military Cemetery.

Joseph Eaton, another local casualty of 'The worst day of the British Army'

The 'Iron Harvest' still kills people - an unexploded shell at Foncquevillers in 2013

Henry was just 21 when he died, the same age as the author (his great-nephew) the first time he visited Foncquevillers on the 70th anniversary of Henry's death in July 1986. This visit was the first of many to the Somme and to Henry's grave and ultimately provided the inspiration for this book, twenty-eight years later.

Alban Eaton
10th Sherwood Foresters, 4th July 1916

Alban was born in 1897, the son of Arthur and Agnes Eaton. The 1911 census finds his parents and siblings at Oxford Road, Ilkeston but Alban is working as a farm labourer in Brailes, Warwickshire with his uncle Alban Alexander.

Alban Eaton enlisted in Derby. He served in the 10th Battalion, the Sherwood Foresters (Notts & Derby) Regiment, one of Kitchener's "new army" regiments, raised from the volunteers of 1914 which shipped out to France in July the following year.

Alban was killed in action on Tuesday 4th July 1916 aged 19, during a reconnaissance mission near Contalmaison in the Somme area, four days after the start of the battle.

His body was never identified, so he is commemorated on the memorial to the missing of the Somme at Thiepval. He is also remembered on the Ilkeston Cenotaph.

Enoch Baker
7th North Staffordshire Regt., 5th October 1916

Enoch was born on 22nd December 1891 in Ilkeston. In the 1911 census he is living with parents John and Lois and four younger siblings at 48 Norman Street. His father was a coal hewer but Enoch's occupation was stated as 'moneylender's clerk'.

He married Lizzie Pick on 5th April 1915 at St John's Church, Ilkeston and on 8th February 1916 they had a daughter, Jessie. Enoch's enlistment record says that he worked as a 'traveller' on enlistment at Mansfield on 11th December 1915. Fortunately, although damaged most of his military records survive to tell the tale of his unfortunate end.

Enoch was lucky not to have joined the 7th North Staffordshires earlier in 1915, when they had a rough time in Gallipoli. By January 1916 they were in Egypt, and by the following month were stationed in Mesopotamia - today's Iraq. Enoch's medical examination is stamped 28th April 1916 and he travelled to meet the regiment shortly afterwards.

On 5th October 1916 Private Baker was in camp near Abu Sidra near Kut in Mesopotamia. The records show that at about 4.45pm he was shot once in the head and died very shortly afterwards. A Court of Inquiry was held on 9th October to establish what had happened, and some of the court's record survives. His death was not suicide.

Witnesses stated that Enoch had been inside his tent with his comrade Private J T Boulton, cleaning his rifle when Boulton heard a sudden shot and Enoch fell to the ground. The shot had not come from Enoch's rifle.

The court heard from a Private Sheppard, servant to an officer, 2nd. Lieut. Hyman. He had been detailed to clean Lieut. Hyman's pistol, which he did, leaving two bullets in the chamber. The pistol was placed in its holster beneath a blanket on Sheppard's bed. After cautioning the men nearby not to touch the loaded revolver, Sheppard went away to wash and while there heard the shot. The pistol had discharged, firing one bullet from inside his tent into the next, where it hit the unfortunate Enoch Baker. Evidence was given that Private H Crewe had been seen handling the revolver while Sheppard was absent. Crewe had been seen taking the pistol from its holster and was arrested. In his defence, Crewe said that he had been lying on his own bed, next to that of Sheppard when Sheppard left. He admitted to taking the revolver out of its holster and holding it in his hand when it went off. He said he did not press the trigger. He said he had never handled a revolver and was 'curious to see how one worked, never having seen one at close quarters before'. He had rushed to the next tent and bound up Enoch's head with a towel. While he was washing the blood from his hands he was arrested.

Frustratingly, the presiding officer has chosen to write the court's opinion in a light blue ink which has perished, so we do not know what penalty if any was suffered by Crewe. Evidently the court believed the accused's explanation as to how Enoch Baker died, as the records state that Enoch was 'accidentally killed'. He was buried on 16th October 1916 near Abu Sidra. His will has survived, in which he left everything to his wife Lizzie of 30 Archer Street, Ilkeston. Sadly, Lizzie found herself having to write a stern and very businesslike letter to the army on 22nd August 1917 as she had still not received her late husband's effects from Iraq. By this time she was living with her mother on Whitworth Road. With typical efficiency, the War Office wrote to their Records Office at Lichfield on 29th July 1918 instructing Enoch's effects to be forwarded to Lizzie at 4 Whitworth Road. The note is endorsed 'Forwarded 20-1-19'.

Although Enoch Baker is now buried in the Amara War Cemetery in Iraq, the Commonwealth War Graves Commission has decided that no maintenance can be carried out due to the unstable political situation. The headstones were removed in the 1930's and when last inspected Enoch's name was one of those remembered on a screen wall which apparently still stands. The CWGC says that it hopes to be able to carry out maintenance before too long.

George Harrison,
1/5th Sherwood Foresters, 7th December 1916

Private 3961 George Harrison was born in 1895; his parents were Thomas, an ironworks fetler (probably at Bennerley Ironworks) and Mary, who lived at 49 Awsworth Road Ilkeston in 1911. He had been a miner in civilian life and when he joined up on 3rd March 1915 aged 19 was living at 14 Lord Haddon Road. George's record shows he officially joined the British Expeditionary Force on 12th October 1915 and that he was killed in action when serving in the trenches near Sus-St-Ledger, France, on Thursday 7th December 1916 when aged 22.

Thiepval Memorial to The Missing

The Thiepval Memorial, the Memorial to the Missing of the Somme, bears the names of more than 72,000 of the United Kingdom and South African forces who died in the Somme sector before 20th March 1918 and have no known grave. Over 90% of these died between July and November 1916.
The memorial, designed by Sir Edwin Lutyens, was built between 1928 and 1932 and was dedicated by the (then) Prince of Wales in the presence of the French President on 1st August 1932.

He is buried in grave I. H. 29. in the Foncquevillers Military Cemetery, Pas de Calais, France, with several other Ilkeston lads and is commemorated on the Ilkeston Cenotaph.

George Ernest Meakin,
HMS *Martial*, 23rd December 1916

George was born in Ilkeston on 22nd August 1886 to George and Sarah. In 1891 they were living with her mother Sarah Richardson at 56 King Street, Ilkeston. By 1901 though, George may have been an orphan as his parents are probably the Sarah and George Meakin who died in 1894 and 1900 respectively. At this time George was living with Frederick Linfield and family at 145 Bath Street and is described as the Linfields' 'adopted son'. His trade is stated to be a grocer's shop boy. The Pioneer says he worked for 'Mr A. Sinfield, butcher' before leaving Ilkeston 'in his youth'.

George signed up for the Navy for twelve years on 12th January 1906 aged 19. Over the next ten years he served on nine ships and some shore installations, starting with HMS *Acheron*, an old three masted stoker training ship. In May 1911 he was promoted to Leading Stoker and in July 1913 to Petty Officer Stoker. He served some time in HMS *Pembroke II*, a shore installation which was one of the Navy's earliest flight schools (later RAF Eastchurch). By the 1911 Census he was aboard HMS *London*, second flagship of the Atlantic Fleet, at Gibraltar. *London* had just finished a major refit and he was one of her new crew on a 'shakedown' cruise. Later, George served aboard HMS *Aboukir*, an obsolete battleship which was famously torpedoed at the start of the war along with HMS *Cressy* and HMS *Hogue*, all three sunk on the same day (see Chapter '1914').

In October 1915 he was posted to a brand new destroyer, HMS *Martial*. Most of his deployments were based in home waters, particularly the south east of England. In the spring of 1910 George married Edith Blanche Holbrook at Sheppey, Kent. They set up a home called 'Ilkeston House' at 30 Coronation Road, Sheerness.

On 23rd December 1916 while serving on *Martial*, George disappeared. His body was never found and a Court of Inquiry decided that he 'presumably fell overboard'. He was treated as a war casualty. Edith received letters of condolence from his shipmates, including Lt. Commander Julian Hamson, who said "Your husband was such a splendid man; always so cheerful and so ready to help everyone at any time that we all feel his sad death as a personal loss and a great blow to the ship".

Lt. Cmdr A W J Turner, one of the ship's engineering officers wrote that "I feel his loss very deeply. He was my store-keeping Petty Officer and I saw a great deal more of him than my other Petty Officers and I, like all who knew him, had a great regard and admiration for him" before hinting that the accidental death was a result of poor maintenance. "He died for his country just as much as those who fell at Jutland, for the state of the ship, due to the war, was indirectly the cause of him falling from the ship".

George was 33 years old and is commemorated on the Chatham Royal Naval Memorial.

Pip, Squeak and Wilfred

Those who joined the war in 1914/15 and fought on the Western Front were awarded the
1914/15 star, the War Medal and the Victory Medal, commonly known as
'Pip, Squeak and Wilfred' after popular cartoon characters of the period.
All of those who fought for the allies were awarded the rainbow-ribboned Victory Medal.

The 'Silver War Badge' awarded to
wounded ex-servicemen

All: Grant Shaw

Sherwood Foresters Cap Badge and (right) the badge of the Church Lads' Brigade
which belonged to Henry Shaw. His mother quoted the CLB motto when writing his epitaph:
"My darling boy. Fought the Good Fight and is rewarded in Heaven. Love Mother".

Brass uniform badge worn
on the shoulder,
identifying the wearer as
a 'Sherwood Forester'.

Chapter Five

1917

More Somme - Army cyclists - Mesopotamia Campaign - Salonika - Death by alcoholic poisoning - Poison gas - Sailors in the Trenches - The sinking of SS Transylvania - Passchendaele

Vincent Horridge,
1/5 Sherwood Foresters, 21st January 1917

Vincent was born in 1890 to William and Mary Ann Horridge. He married Sarah J Baxter from Greasley in late 1910, but sadly she died not long afterwards. She is probably the Sarah J Horridge whose death was recorded in Nottingham registration district aged 19 in the early months of 1911.

Their daughter Hephzibah had been born in the summer of 1909 before the marriage and what was bluntly called a 'bastardy order' had been obtained against Vincent (presumably by her parents as Sarah would have been only 17) which obliged him to pay seven shillings and sixpence a week towards his daughter's upkeep.

In 1911 as a widower he was living back with his parents at 13 Belvoir Street Ilkeston and like his father, his occupation in the census is stated to be that of a coal miner.

Vincent joined up on 4th November 1914. His army records survive, and this is why we have some detail about his life. The enlistment record says he was a Baptist; he served in the British Isles first then on 22nd April 1916 he was transferred to 1/5 Sherwood Foresters on arriving in France. Vincent survived the Somme in which so many other local soldiers died, but was killed in action on 21st January 1917. He is buried in the Foncquevillers Military Cemetery in Pas-de-Calais not far from the town of Albert with several other Ilkeston men who died in 1916 and 1917.

Interestingly, Vincent's army will has survived and is available to view online. This was written on one page of his paybook and is dated 30th April 1916. The will leaves everything to his father William.

The army made enquiries of the Derbyshire Constabulary regarding Vincent's daughter and his army record contains a letter from Superintendent Charles Walker on 28th September 1917 confirming the details of the Court Order. Vincent's daughter was awarded an allowance of seven shillings a week from 28th August 1917, which was paid to her guardian. In 1919 she was living in Newthorpe with her Baxter relatives.

By this time Vincent's father was also a widower. William received his son's personal effects well after the event, and these consisted only of an identity disc, a pipe (broken), a knife and belt. William complained that he had not received his son's silk handkerchief, but there is no record that this was ever returned.

George Wood poses with his anxious
mother before going off to war

Clarence Gordon Shaw

David Hudson

Thomas Hooley (left) and pals show off their new uniforms

Hephzibah (from Hebrew - translated as 'my delight is in her') is an uncommon name and Vincent's daughter might be the Hephzibah Baxter who married Isaiah Atkins at Tamworth in the spring of 1930 aged 21.

Frank Aldwinckle
7th Prince of Wales's (North Staffordshire) Regt., 25th January 1917

Frank's father Cecil was born in Northamptonshire and his trade in the 1891 census is stated as 'sinker'. Mother Frances Amelia was born in West Hallam and her occupation was as a dressmaker. The family of seven including six year-old Frank were then living at 111 Bath Street.

Ten years later and the family are living at 76 Station Road. Cecil is now a coal hewer but this census says (incorrectly) that all the family were born in Ilkeston including parents. At 16, Frank is also working down the pit as a coal hewer.

By 1911 Frank is one of only two children still living at 76 Station Road and he is still a miner although the census describes him as 'injured'. We cannot say what his injuries were but this didn't stop him being called up and he joined the army in June 1916.

He was sent to the 7th North Staffordshires. The regimental history, published in 1932 records that even by the standards of the British army the regiment had a reputation for its profanity. When the 1st Battalion was relieved in the front line at Delville Wood in September 1916, one of the advanced posts was missed out by mistake. The lance corporal in command, suspecting something was wrong, sent a soldier back to the front line trench to investigate. The man realised he was at risk of being shot by his own side, so

> "when he had crawled within shouting distance he enquired politely but firmly what f****** b******s were holding that f****** trench. The 9th East Surreys, who were the troops thus addressed, recognised the North Stafford idiom and let him in unhurt,"

December 1916 found them engaging the Ottoman (Turkish) Army in what is now Iraq. Frank wrote home to his mother and father :

> "Our company has been marching and resting at times and we have now got to the trenches, within gunshot of the Turks. I have been sick for about three weeks with dysentery, but am now about right again, and hope to keep so.
>
> It has been raining, and things get very damp, but we are hoping to make things more comfortable when we get settled down, as we have to do a lot of moving about from one camp to another, so I don't have much time. When I was at the rest camp a lot of the North Staffords went forward and fell in with the Turks and took some prisoners, but they lost __ wounded and __ killed. We passed Christmas all right, and we got a piece of cake and pudding and also a glass of rum the next day, so under such conditions we must not grumble too much,"

On January 25th 1917 Frank was killed in action. He was 31 and is commemorated on the Basra Memorial in Iraq. This large and impressive memorial, which once stood on the banks of the Shatt-el-Arab waterway near Basra was famously and at no small effort relocated and renovated on the personal orders of Saddam Hussein in 1997.

Frank is also commemorated on his parents' monument in Park Cemetery, Ilkeston.

Harold Barker
6th King's Own (Royal Lancaster) Regiment, 13th February 1917

Harold Barker was 27 years and 9 months old when he volunteered for the army on 30th August 1915. A hosiery hand, he was living with his widowed mother Mary Ann and seven of his siblings on North Street, Ilkeston at the time of the 1911 census.

As you have heard, the Army Service Records for the Great War were heavily damaged and many were lost in the London Blitz. Over the last few years many which were thought to be irretrievably damaged have in fact been reconstructed from what was left - they were known as the 'burnt' records and have now been digitised and are available online. It is pot luck how much is left and whether anything is left at all, but Harold's record bears scorch marks and has been burned around the edges, meaning that only the centre of each page was saved (This leads the author to suspect that the records were archived after the Great War in bales, with blocks of them wrapped with string or similar).

What is left tells us that Harold joined the Sherwood Foresters but was transferred to the 3rd and later 6th Battalion the King's Own Royal Lancaster Regiment whom he joined in May 1916 as a Private. The King's Own had just come back from Gallipoli and were stationed in Egypt for a while. Harold caught up with them in Mesopotamia, landing at Basra on 13th June 1916.

Harold arrived just after a long period of fighting in which the 13th Division had won three Victoria Crosses in the previous three months and were now preparing to push north east towards Baghdad. On 5th September 1916 he was admitted to hospital. This may not have been due to fighting, as his division was re-equipping at the time. Harold was discharged back to his unit eleven days later.

His unit fought at the Second Battle of Kut, a town which had been first taken by the British and then recaptured by the Ottomans the previous year.

They then pressed on with their march towards Baghdad but Harold was shot on 13th February and was admitted to hospital 'dangerously wounded' with a gunshot wound in his right arm and fractured right leg. He died later that day. He was 29 years old. Harold is buried in the Amara War Cemetery in Iraq.

William Herbert Straw
No. 2 Special Battalion, Royal Engineers, 5th April 1917

Herbert, as he was known, was born in late 1896 in Clapham, London to parents William Barker Straw (born in West Hallam) and Louisa Straw (born in Ilkeston). His father was a general furniture dealer and his parents obviously lived in London for at least four years until Herbert's birth.

By the 1901 census they are back in Ilkeston at 20 Granby Street, where they stayed. In 1901 they have a domestic servant living-in but not in the 1911 census. At 14 Herbert is down as a 'draper's assistant' in 1911 and his father's occupation has changed to 'draper'. Father and son worked together.

Herbert applied to join the Army Cyclist Corps on 30th October 1915 and was accepted four days later at the training centre at Hounslow, Middlesex. Various Cyclist units had been formed from the 1880s onwards and by 1915 they had been largely amalgamated into the Army Cyclist Corps. It may seem odd today, but in a world without suitable all terrain vehicles the bicycle could prove a very useful aid to reconnaissance. It was not, though, much use in the trenches which is why most cyclists served at home until almost the end of the war when the trench system had been broken.

His medical record shows that Herbert was hospitalised for a few days at the beginning of April 1916 with influenza, but he was soon discharged. At the end of that month while in Rouen, perhaps while recuperating he was fined some days pay as a result of a minor deficiency in his kit (the records are not clear). Perhaps as a result of this, Herbert applied for a transfer to the Royal Engineers as a Pioneer. This was accepted in June 1916. He joined No. 2 Special Battalion, which was one of the units responsible for administering poison gas as an offensive weapon.

On 11th April 1917 his father received a telegram from the Royal Engineers at Brompton Barracks, Chatham informing him baldly "Regret to inform you Officer Commanding 11th Canadian Field Ambulance France reports 6th April 156585 H W Straw RE died of wounds (date not stated). Colonel in charge RE Records". A later telegram confirmed that Herbert had died of wounds on 5th April 1917. He was 20.

The Ilkeston Pioneer reported on 13th April that

> "The deceased soldier was only 19 [sic] years of age but had been out in France eleven months. He was attached to the Royal Engineers and was assisting his brother, Stephen Henry, who is a chemist and 25 years of age, in the work of discharging gas in the direction of the German trenches, when an enemy shell fell amongst a party of them, and he was either killed instantly or so badly wounded that he dies shortly afterwards, his brother having the gruesome task of carrying his body to the casualty station.
>
> Private Straw was acting as an assistant to his father when he enlisted and had previously been in a boot shop in Nottingham,"

David Johnson Barber

Frank Aldwinckle

Michael Talbot

Leonard Boden Shipstone in a jolly souvenir taken in Ilkeston before
leaving for France. He and his brother Percy are remembered on
their parents' grave in Greasley churchyard.

David Johnson Barber
7th Ox & Bucks Light Infantry, 7th April 1917

David was born on February 18th 1886 at Hallam Fields, the only son of William and Ruth Barber who later kept the White Hart Inn at West Hallam. The 1891 census shows him there aged five with two older sisters. The White Hart was also a farm at this time and two farm labourers and a domestic servant lived with the family.

Ten years later, David's circumstances had changed substantially. After starting his education at the Scargill School in West Hallam under Headmaster Mr Raby, he was in 1901 a boarder at Bablake Grammar, a private school in Coventry founded in 1344 and thus one of the oldest schools in the United Kingdom. It seems likely that he may have won a scholarship, but in any case at the time of the census he was the only pupil living with the Headmaster's family in their own house. While at Bablake he became friends with William Leefe Robinson, who won a Victoria Cross in the War for being the first to shoot down a Zeppelin airship over Britain.

David was a keen cricketer, playing for West Hallam White Rose Cricket Club. By the 1911 census, he was living as a boarder with the Wass family at Bridge Foot, Belper and was working as a cashier for the Nottingham Joint Stock Bank, whom he had joined in 1905. In the spring of 1911 he married Lilian Joyce Beresford and they settled down in Belper.

David joined the Royal Field Artillery in May 1916, but was transferred to the Royal Sussex Regiment and then to the Oxfordshire & Buckinghamshire Light Infantry as a Private.

When David joined them in October 1916, the 'Ox and Bucks' were in the 'Happy Valley' Camp in the region they called Salonika (Thessaloniki) in Greece where they had fought the Bulgarians (allies of Germany) in the Battle of Horseshoe Hill earlier in 1916. Apart from this, their time in Salonika appears to have been fairly uneventful with only sporadic fighting.

However, the records show that David died of wounds on 7th April 1917, just before his regiment was involved in the Battle of Doiran in present day FYR Macedonia. The news reached his family some days later, on Easter Monday.

He was aged 31 and left a widow and two young children. The Ilkeston Pioneer said he was "of a kind and affectionate disposition, and was very popular amongst his large circle of friends" and said that both Lily and his parents had received a "large number of sympathetic letters".

David's body was buried in the Salonika (Lembet Road) Military Cemetery, to the north of the modern Greek city of Thessaloniki which has now grown around it.

His will left everything to his widow Lilian and his estate was valued at £240 13s. 7d. His name appears on the Bablake School Memorial and on the West Hallam War Memorial.

John Hendy
Prince of Wales's (North Staffordshire) Regiment, 15th April 1917

John was born in 1893 to Isaiah and Eliza. His father had been born in Worcestershire and was one of many who moved to the area when they found work at the thriving Stanton Ironworks. The family lived on Crompton Street, Hallam Fields. The 1911 Census finds John boarding with the Gordon family at 70 Crompton Street and he is employed as a shunter at Stanton.

John joined the 10th (Training) Battalion of the Sherwood Foresters in November 1915. We know nothing of his service for the next year or so as his record has been heavily water damaged. On 15th March 1917 he married Lily Borhand at Ilkeston's Congregational Church.

He was transferred to the Prince of Wales's (North Staffordshire) Regiment in February 1917 and set sail from Southampton for France shortly afterwards. Boarding the troopship *Cameronia* at Marseilles, he set off to complete his journey to Alexandria. The *Cameronia* was a 10,963 ton Anchor Line two-funnel passenger liner launched in 1911 and which had been employed on the cross Atlantic route to New York before being requisitioned as a troop transport.

On 15th April 1917 when she was 150 miles east of Malta the *Cameronia* was torpedoed by German submarine *U-33*. There were approximately 2,650 soldiers on board and the ship sank in no more than forty minutes. The death toll could have been much worse; only 210 lives were lost but one of these was Private John Hendy. He had been married exactly one month.

It was not until 27th October that the authorities officially declared him dead. His body was never identified so he is commemorated on the Chatby Memorial in Alexandria, Egypt. Some of the *Cameronia*'s survivors were treated in hospital in Malta by Edwin Jeffery and had their photograph taken with him - this is reprinted later in this book (see 'After').

Albert Potter
1/5 Sherwood Foresters, 18th April 1917

Albert was born in the first quarter of 1891, the brother of Thomas Edward and James Henry (see 1914). The 1911 census finds him with parents James and Mary and three of his five siblings living at 14 Brussells Terrace, Ilkeston. He was employed as a Coal Miner (loader).

He joined the Sherwood Foresters in March 1915, and although it is not known when he landed in France he was fighting with the 1/5 by March 1916. It is not clear whether he attacked with the rest of the 1/5th on 1st July 1916 at Gommecourt, but in any case, he survived the Battle of the Somme.

On 18th April 1917 Albert and two other men under supervision of a Lance Corporal Harrison were set to work moving timber to new positions on a slag heap in the mining area near the old battlefield of Loos. Harrison and Private Herbert Bollington went to look into an abandoned German dugout and found a British stone jar containing about three pints of what they believed to be rum. No rum had been issued to the men that day, and Harrison took the jar to the others.

They all had a drink, Harrison and Albert having rather more than the rest. They settled down under a railway bridge, where time passed and more was drunk.

Eventually they were missed. A party sent to find them found Albert and Harrison on the railway line, with the other two in a dugout on top of the railway bank. The Corporal and Albert had passed out and the others were heavily overcome with drink. Albert was sick and it soon became clear that he was actually very ill indeed.

Albert was soon comatose. Lance Corporal Yeomans borrowed a truck from the railway men and collected him and Lance Corporal Harrison, taking Albert to hospital. Yeomans said that all the men smelt strongly of rum. By the time they had arrived at the hospital, Albert was dead.

At the Court of Enquiry held into his death the next day 'in the field', Captain Campbell Suttie, a Doctor from the hospital confirmed that Albert had been dead when he arrived at the hospital, that the body smelt strongly of rum and that this and the pallor of the body indicated that the cause of death was "syncope which would have been caused by acute alcohol poisoning".

After taking evidence from the principal parties, the Court (including Ilkeston Solicitor Lieutenant F.G. Robinson, who had taken Albert's original attestation on joining the army) found Lance Corporal Harrison to be to blame for allowing rum to be drunk while on duty. A Court Martial was ordered and confirmed by the Major General commanding the 46th Division on 25th April.

There is a note attached to Albert's records to say that disciplinary action was being taken against L/Cpl Harrison but that he 'became a casualty during the action of 1st July, 1917'. Interestingly, the CWGC records do not show a fatality which matches him, so we can only assume he must have been captured or injured rather than killed.

Albert was 26 when he died, and is buried in the Maroc British Cemetery at Grenay, near the French/Belgian border.

Fred Chaplin
Royal Army Medical Corps, 4th May 1917

Fred was born in June 1895 to George and Zillah who had both been born in Bedworth, Warwickshire. Before moving to Ilkeston, George's work as a coal hewer had taken them to Bestwood, Barnsley and Masborough before settling in Ilkeston six years before Fred was born. He was the youngest of eight children.

By the 1911 census, Zillah had died and George had married Mary Rose. Her son and daughter are living with the Chaplins at 92 Lord Haddon Road, and Fred (like almost every other male worker in the town) was a coal miner. He worked at the West Hallam Colliery and is said to have studied mining with a view to taking a manager's qualification. Fred was a Primitive Methodist and a staunch teetotaller.

Fred joined the Ilkeston Ambulance Corps in the summer of 1913 and enlisted in the Royal Army Medical Corps on 18th November 1914. He was stationed in a military hospital in Brighton and received a certificate for his 'medical efficiency'. On April 1st 1917 he returned home on leave before departing for France on 18th. From France he was posted to Egypt and took ship at Marseille on the SS *Transylvania,* a passenger liner operated by the Cunard subsidiary Anchor Line bound for Alexandria and which was escorted by the Japanese destroyers *Matsu* and *Sakaki.*

At 10am on 4th May the *Transylvania* was struck in the port engine room by a torpedo fired by the German submarine *U-63.* At the time the ship was just under three miles south of Cape Vado near Savona, not far from the city of Genoa on the north-west coast of Italy. The *Matsu* came alongside and began to take on board troops while the *Sakaki* circled to force the submarine to remain submerged.

Twenty minutes later a second torpedo was seen coming straight for the *Matsu,* which saved herself by going astern at full speed. The torpedo hit the *Transylvania* instead, and she sank immediately. Ten crew members, 29 army officers and 373 soldiers lost their lives.

Many bodies of victims were recovered at Savona and buried two days later in a special plot in the town cemetery. Others are buried elsewhere in Italy, France, Monaco and Spain. Inside the cemetery is the Savona Memorial which commemorates a further 275 casualties who died when the *Transylvania* sank, but whose graves are unknown. One such is Fred Chaplin. He was three weeks away from his 22nd birthday.

Also lost on the *Transylvania* was Driver Henry Bostock of the Royal Army Service Corps, whose parents lived at 17 Byron Street. He was 25 and had enlisted in the winter of 1915. He too is commemorated on the Savona Memorial.

Another local soldier involved in the sinking was Private Sam Kidger of Station Road, Ilkeston who survived. He sent a letter to his sister which was printed in the Ilkeston Pioneer :

"No doubt you will have seen by now which ship I was on. It was a very large one. When the first torpedo hit her I was down below, and it put all the lights out. When I got out on deck some of the boats were leaving the ship with the nurses on board.

A Japanese Torpedo Boat Destroyer had just drawn alongside and was taking men off when I saw a second torpedo coming through the water, and that was worse than the first. Then the order was every man overboard. It was awful. We could not launch any more boats. The rafts we threw overboard to the men in the water. I was on the point of jumping in also.

I had taken my boots and puttees off when I saw a second JTBD coming alongside and I jumped on to her as she was passing by and I might say there were hundreds saved like that, all honour to the Japs, they are brave men. I also saw men fall between both ships and were crushed to death. I shall never forget it.

I got off ten minutes before she sank. I am pleased to say we landed in sunny Italy, and the people gave us a great welcome. They gave us wine, ciggs, cigars and such beautiful flowers and I had to walk through the town barefooted. Now we are again in France in the place we started from [Marseille]."

We shall hear more of Sam Kidger later.

Leonard Boden Shipstone, Royal Field Artillery, 18th May 1917
Percy Shipstone, Cheshire Regiment, 23rd June 1917

Percy Shipstone was born in 1889 and his younger brother Leonard in 1896 in Eastwood. Their parents were Edward Shipstone (a colliery banksman) and his wife the former Elizabeth Boden Mellor, daughter of William Mellor, a butcher on South Street, Ilkeston. By 1911 they had five other siblings and the family was living at Nottingham Road, Giltbrook. In the 1911 census when aged 14 Leonard is stated to be an 'errand boy' and Percy at 21 is a 'grocer's assistant'. Percy (whom the family called 'Poss') went on to be Grocery Manager and Buyer at the Co-operative shop at Woodborough, Nottingham. He married Mabel Hodgkinson in April 1915.

Percy joined up on 11th December 1915. Although he joined the Sherwood Foresters he was posted to the Cheshire Regiment and underwent training at Rugeley. By 3rd May 1917 he was fighting with the Cheshires in France.

Leonard joined the Royal Field Artillery. He was a tall lad, and this posed a problem as the army initially couldn't find a uniform which would fit him. He underwent training at the Deepcut Camp in Hampshire and sent at least one letter home to his mother, ending with the words "Absence makes the love grow stronger".

Posted to the 402nd Battery, RFA Len was sent to fight in France, rising slightly in rank to that of 'fitter'. He was wounded on 26th April 1917, probably in the battle for Vimy Ridge as his unit were attached to the Canadian Army attacking there. He was sent back to a General Hospital on the coast with severe leg injuries. One of Len's friends, a Bombardier H. Eyre, wrote to his parents to reassure them :

"... your son Len ... got a slight wound in the leg yesterday. Len asked me to drop you a note to tell you all not to worry too much for he would soon be better. He may get to England with it and he thought ... you would have worried about him. I am a friend of your son and I hope he will soon [regain?]. Please let me [know] when he get a letter to you my address is the same as his. Hoping to hear from you, I remain your son's friend H. Eyre"

On 27th April Len managed to send out one of the short pro-forma cards on which the Army only allowed the briefest of messages, saying that he had "been admitted to hospital and was going on well".

Percy managed to get leave to go and see Leonard. When he arrived on 18th May 1917, he was told that his younger brother had died earlier that day. Percy wrote a letter home to his mother and father, which has survived.

Leonard Boden Shipstone

Both : Christine Allen and Don Boden Chambers

Percy ('Poss') and Mabel Shipstone

78

"The Sister told me he passed away at 12pm last night and she thought he knew he was dying. He asked for his mother, Jim and Ethel. I don't know who Jim is but most probably it would be his chum so perhaps in the course of the next few days he will be writing you. [...] It was the shock of my life when the sister told me the news, but she said his left leg would have been 6 or 8 inches shorter than the other had he lived, but I would sooner him have lived than died as he has done. If God spares me to come back I shall be able to tell you all the news, so cheer up dear mother and don't trouble to much he has died a noble death and I know he has gone to heaven. Someday we shall all be able to meet him and what a gathering it will be. I must now close I can't bear to write any more. I will write you more details when I get settled down a little more. So good-bye and God bless you all. Ever your loving son, Poss. xxxxxxxxxxxx"

Percy went back to his unit and fought at Messines Ridge. On 7th June 1917 he was seriously injured with gunshot wounds in the back. Percy too was sent back to a General Hospital at Camiers near the coast where he died on 23rd June, just over a month after his younger brother Leonard. Percy was 28.

Leonard and Percy are buried not too far apart in the huge Commonwealth War Cemetery at Etaples. In 1917 the area around Etaples contained several hospitals including eleven general, one 'stationary' hospital, four Red Cross hospitals and a convalescent depot, which together could deal with 22,000 wounded or sick. The cemetery contains 10,771 Commonwealth burials of the First World War, the earliest dating from May 1915. This cemetery, the largest CWGC cemetery in France, was designed by Sir Edwin Lutyens.

Both brothers are commemorated on their parents' grave in Greasley Churchyard. Percy's widow Mabel was awarded 13 shillings and 9 pence a week pension. After the war, she visited Percy's grave. Mabel remarried in 1931 and died in 1973 aged 85.

George Wood,
2nd Sherwood Foresters, 1st July 1917

George was born in 1896/7 in Trowell. By the 1901 census he, his parents and ten siblings were living at 77 Trowell Moor, and his father's occupation was stated as 'farmer'. Although both his parents and most of his younger siblings were born in Trowell, his family had moved around as one brother was born in Sheffield, and another in Ilkeston. By 1911 they were living at 24 Brooke Street Ilkeston and his occupation (at age 14) was stated as "learning crane driving", his older brother William (16) being a crane driver.

It is not clear when George joined the 2nd Battalion the Sherwood Foresters but he was killed on 1st July 1917. His body was not identified and he is commemorated on the impressive Loos Memorial on the French border with Belgium. The walls around the large cemetery contain the names of the missing - George's appears in one of the right hand pavilions at the rear along with his pals from the Notts & Derby Regiment.

The CWCG records state that his mother lived at 21 French Street, Ilkeston when these were compiled in the 1920's. We have printed a photograph of George and his mother Alice (nee Adkin) taken about 1916.

Reginald Corns,
Royal Field Artillery, 13th August 1917

Reg's father Albert was born in Tipton, Staffordshire and he moved to Derbyshire to work in the ironmaking industry. He married Kate Townsend and they had three sons.

Reginald was born at Riddings, Derbyshire in 1896, the year before the family moved to new housing at Crompton Street, Hallam Fields. Sadly his mother Kate died around the year 1900. The year after, with young children to support, Albert married again to widow Marian Botham. They had a further eight children.

Reg joined the Church Lads' Brigade and became an iron-moulder at Stanton Ironworks. He enlisted in the Royal Field Artillery in 1914 at the Traveller's Rest Pub on White Lion Square (known jokingly at the time as the 'War Office').

A romantic involvement with Rose Ethel Jones, two years his junior led to a son, Harry. When Harry's birth was registered on March 2nd, 1916, the name of the father was not entered on the certificate. Reg and Rose married at Long Eaton Registry Office on March 13th, 1917. Very soon after, Reg was back on the front line in Belgium.

Reg was killed in Belgium on the 13th August 1917, during the Battle of Passchendaele, also called the Third Battle of Ypres. He is buried in the New Irish Farm Cemetery, St Jean-Les-Ypres, Belgium. This cemetery was opened in August 1917 and had previously been just a series of front line trenches. After the Armistice, the cemetery was enlarged with the concentration of 4,560 graves adding to the 70 already there.

Reg was one of the first soldiers to have been buried in this cemetery, and his grave occupies a raised place in the centre of the plot.

Reuben Shaw
HMS *Europa*, 11th September 1917

Reuben was born on Bonfire Night, 5th November 1895, the second son of Reuben and Mary of Carr Street. His father died when Reuben was only three years old and he was adopted by his uncle and aunt James and Georgina Cooke of Station Road, Ilkeston.

Working in his uncle's business "James Cooke and Son", whom the Pioneer described as 'marine store dealers' but were probably better known as scrap metal merchants, Reuben eventually became a partner and manager.

Paul Miller

THE TRAGEDY OF
HMS *BULWARK*

Bulwark was moored off Sheerness on 26th November 1914. While most of the crew were having breakfast, the ship was blown apart by a powerful explosion .

Herbert Saunders Nunn, a career sailor born in Ilkeston was one of 736 men who died.

A Court of Inquiry found that the explosion had been caused not by the enemy but by either faulty handling or storage of *Bulwark*'s own ammunition.

The disaster remains the second most catastrophic accidental explosion in the history of the United Kingdom.

Top left : The Portsmouth Naval Memorial
Centre Left : Herbert Saunders Nunn
Bottom Left : Herbert's name on the memorial

HMS *Bulwark*

Image © Imperial War Museum (Q21052B)

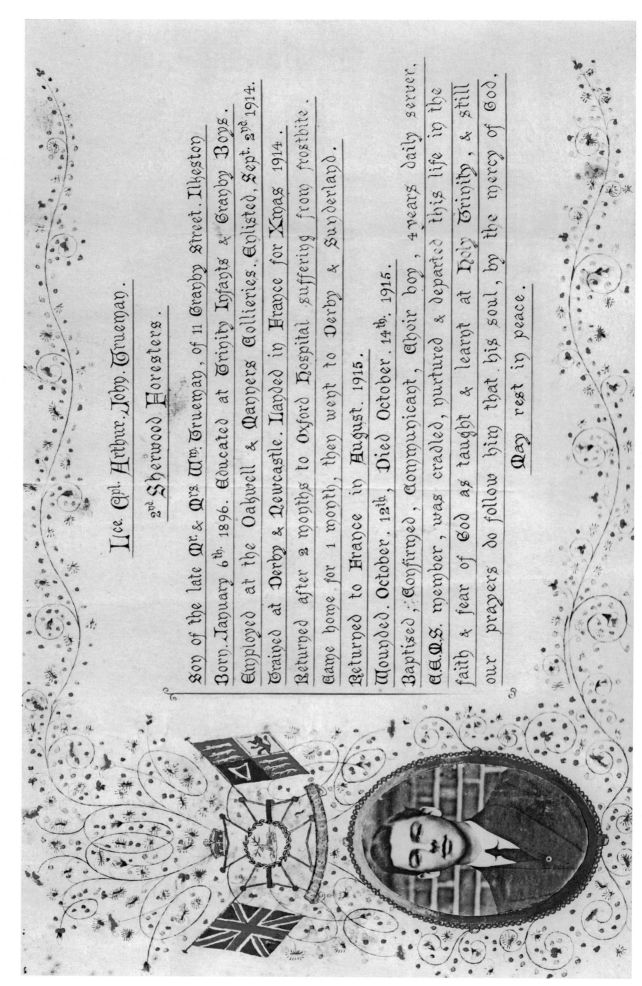

Lce. Cpl. Arthur. John. Trueman.

2ⁿᵈ Sherwood Foresters.

Son of the late Mr. & Mrs. Wᵐ. Trueman, of 11 Cranby Street. Ilkeston.
Born. January 6ᵗʰ. 1896. Educated at Trinity Infants & Cranby Boys.
Employed at the Oakwell & Manners Collieries. Enlisted, Sept. 2ⁿᵈ. 1914.
Trained at Derby & Newcastle. Landed in France for Xmas 1914.
Returned after 2 months to Oxford Hospital suffering from frostbite.
Came home for 1 month, then went to Derby & Sunderland.
Returned to France in August. 1915.
Wounded. October. 12ᵗʰ. Died October. 14ᵗʰ. 1915.
Baptised ; Confirmed, Communicant, Choir boy, 4 years daily server,
C.E.M.S. member, was cradled, nurtured & departed this life in the
faith & fear of God as taught & learnt at Holy Trinity, & still
our prayers do follow him that his soul, by the mercy of God,

May rest in peace.

A beautifully hand decorated memorial to Arthur John Trueman found in the records of Holy Trinity Church, Ilkeston by David Hudson

II

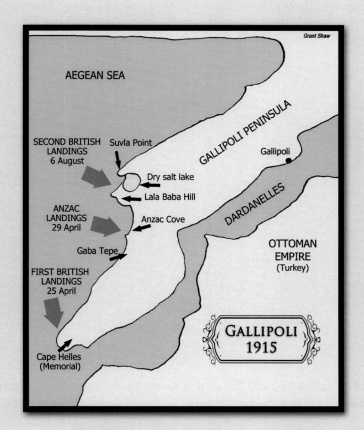

GALLIPOLI AND THE DARDANELLES 1915

Attacking Germany's ally the Ottoman Empire seemed a good way of diverting enemy resources from the Western Front. The attack, championed by First Lord of the Admiralty Winston Churchill, was intended to open the Dardanelles to allied ships making a route to Russia as well as perhaps capturing the Ottoman capital Istanbul.

Almost nothing went right with the campaign. The Turks proved to be a formidable enemy and the attacks both by sea and land were poorly planned and executed, resulting in large numbers of casualties.

The Ottoman forces were led by experienced commanders, a few of whom were German. One of the most able Turkish commanders was Mustafa Kemal, now known as Ataturk who would go on to help found and be the first President of the Republic of Turkey.

By 9th January 1916 all allied troops had been evacuated. During the campaign the allies lost almost 188,000 men, the Ottoman Empire about 175,000.

The crew of HMS *Triumph* inspect deck damage caused by Ottoman Turkish shells in the Dardanelles.
Is Stoker Petty Officer John Waite one of these men?   Image © Imperial War Museum (SP2461)

Mudros Harbour (South) by Frank H. Mason - Copyright (c) Imperial War Museum (Art. IWM ART 3129)

Mudros Bay on the Isle of Lemnos, Greece - The flagship HMS *Europa* is in the centre. Reuben Shaw died on her in 1917 and is buried nearby. The armistice with the Ottoman Empire was signed on *Europa* here in October 1918.

Grant Shaw

The Military Cemetery at Etaples (known as "Eat-apples"), about fifteen miles south of Boulogne -
There were sixteen hospitals in close proximity and this is the largest CWGC cemetery in France.
Several servicemen from the Ilkeston area are buried here.

HOSPITAL SHIP
STOPPED AND SEARCHED
BY A U-BOAT

Albert Cade MM was an orderly with the
Royal Army Medical Corps and he served
in Malta, Egypt, Canada, France,
Belgium and Ireland during the war.

He also served on the Hospital Ship *Essequibo*,
a converted liner which was off the Irish Coast
on the way back to England with wounded
from the Mediterranean on 15th March 1917
when it was forced to stop and was boarded
by a party from Imperial German Navy
Submarine *U-54*, which had been about
to torpedo the steamer before realising
that she was a hospital ship.

The Germans allowed the Essequibo to
proceed after inspecting her, wishing the ship
a 'good voyage' before going on to sink
a 2200 ton French sailing ship later that day.

Above : U54 approaches the ship
Below : The Boarding Party

Above : The HS Essequibo
Below : Satisfied, U54 moves off

Plugstreet

The Ploegsteert Memorial on the Ypres to Armentieres road in southern Belgium.

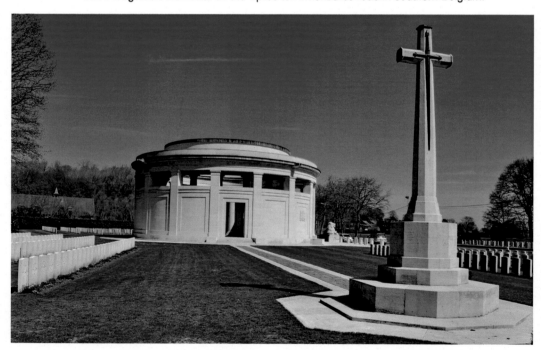

The memorial commemorates more than 11,000 servicemen of the United Kingdom and
South African forces who died in this sector during the First World War and have no known grave.
It adjoins the Berks Cemetery Extension in which Ilkeston's Bombardier E B Johnson is buried.

The Menin Gate Memorial at Ieper (Ypres) in Flanders was dedicated in 1927 and commemorates 54,896 allied combatants who have no known grave. Intended to commemorate all the missing of the Belgian war, in the end this massive memorial proved too small to fit all the names and so another memorial was created at Tyne Cot for those who were missing after August 1917.

No. 314472. Gunner Jack Mather
Royal Field Artillery

Served with honour and was disabled in the Great War.

Honourably discharged on 17th January 1919.

George R.I.

VIII

Cossall War Memorial

Reuben Shaw

Reginald Corns

New Irish Farm Cemetery, Ieper (Ypres)
where Reg Corns is buried

He joined the Royal Navy Volunteer Reserve on 21st November 1916 and spent some time at the Navy Depot at Crystal Palace before being posted to HMS *Vivid*, a training establishment at Devonport, Plymouth. On 20th July 1917 he was posted as an 'Ordinary Seaman' to HMS *Pelorus*, a cruiser supporting operations against Turkey from Greece.

Reuben developed pneumonia around the time he was transferred to the cruiser HMS *Europa* on 25th August 1917. He died of this on 11th September 1917, aged 21 and is buried in East Mudros Military Cemetery on the island of Limnos (Lemnos) in the north-east Aegean Sea.

The Ilkeston Pioneer said that notice of his death reached Mr and Mrs Cooke only three days later.

> "Shaw was small in stature, but was remarkably well developed, and as a footballer he played with the Newdigate and other local teams. Whilst stationed at the Crystal Palace, he was connected with the Seaman Ratings Football Club, winners of the R.N. Depot (Crystal Palace) F.C. 1917 [sic].
>
> He was also in the front rank for wrestling, boxing and swimming. As a boxer, a challenge was issued at the Crystal Palace that he would meet anyone his weight and height, but although the offer was continued for three weeks, it was not accepted. Shaw was well known in the town, and his unexpected death had occasioned a feeling of sorrow amongst his relatives and many friends".

Hezekiah Scattergood
Able Seaman, RNVR, 13th September 1917

We are fortunate that as one of the sailors who fought on the Western Front, Hezekiah's Royal Naval Volunteer Reserve service record is preserved in the National Archives, unlike many of his comrades in the British Army.

He was born on 18th September 1897 (his service record says 21st September 1896) in the Station Road area of Ilkeston and by the 1911 census was living with his parents Lewis and Elizabeth (nee Oakes) and four of his seven surviving siblings at Digby Street, Ilkeston Junction. Although only 13, he was already working underground as a pony driver in a local pit. Sadly his father Lewis died later that year. Hezekiah enlisted in the Navy on 9th November 1915 and was drafted into the Howe Battalion of the Royal Naval Division who were fighting on the Western Front in August 1916.

On 13th November he received a serious gunshot wound to his face which damaged his left eye and he was taken via a casualty clearing station to hospital in Rouen. His injury being judged to be a 'Blighty one' he was sent to Tooting Military Hospital, London. Recovery was slow and he was eventually discharged from hospital on 17th February 1917.

After a couple of weeks' leave he returned to duty with the Navy at a shore depot and was then drafted back into the Howe Battalion of the British Expeditionary Force on 22nd April 1917.

Back in the front line, Hezekiah survived until 13th September 1917, when he was one of four men killed by a German 'pineapple' grenade exploding in his trench.

He was buried in an isolated grave by his comrades, the service being conducted by a Rev. J. McCardel. Hezekiah was 20 years old. In the months of fighting which followed his grave was lost and he is now commemorated on the Arras Memorial, as well on the Cossall War Memorial in St Catherine's Church.

John 'Jack' Syson
2/5 Sherwood Foresters, 3rd October 1917

Jack was born in July 1881 and christened on Christmas Day that year at Cotmanhay Parish Church. In the 1891 census his parents William, a miner, and Hannah plus their six children were living at 20 Prince Street, Cotmanhay.

He joined the St John Ambulance Brigade and served as an Orderly during the South African War (1899-1902) attached to the 20th Bearer Company of the Royal Army Medical Corps. Jack was present at the Battles of Johannesberg, Diamond Hill and Wittebergen in the Cape Colony. He was awarded the South Africa Campaign Medal with clasps and returned to civilian life soon after the war.

The 1911 census finds him living at 43 Milton Road, Cotmanhay with wife of nine years Rebecca and children Dorothy, Mary and John. Jack is working as a 'coal miner /contractor (underground)'.

Jack was recalled to service, this time in the Sherwood Foresters as a corporal and landed in France on 1st March 1915. He was later promoted to Sergeant.

Some time after February 1917 he was transferred to the 2/5 Sherwood Foresters, perhaps at the time of his promotion. This battalion had recently returned from Ireland where they had been used in the suppression of the 'Easter Rising' of 1916 and its aftermath.

His time with the 2/5 was to be short, as on 3rd October 1917 he was killed in action. Jack is buried in the Mendinghem Military Cemetery which is north west of Poperinghe in West Flanders, Belgium.

Francis Leonard Hunter Jackson,
Royal Naval Division, 26th October 1917

Born in Ilkeston on 29th September 1891 to parents Charles John and Agnes Mary Jackson, Francis attended the private boys school St Cuthbert's College, (now known as Worksop College) in Worksop, an Anglican school whose aim was and still is to provide education based on "sound principle and sound knowledge, firmly grounded in the Christian faith".

IN LOVING MEMORY OF

SERGT. JOHN SYSON,

(5th Sherwood Foresters,)

The Beloved Husband of Rebecca Syson,

Who Died on Oct. 3rd, of wounds received in action, Sept. 26, 1917.

AGED THIRTY-SEVEN YEARS.

———

FOR HIS COUNTRY'S SAKE.

———

Though far from his home in a soldier's grave
In memory he'll live for aye.
The evening star shines on the grave
Of one we loved but could not save

Memorial card for Jack Syson

84

His school records show that he did well there, winning the prestigious "Headmaster's Prize" and also the Classics Prize, and on the sporting front he won a swimming certificate and came fourth in the Dormitory Run (a cross-country race which still takes place). He also took part in drama, playing the role of Anne Page in a school production of "The Merry Wives of Windsor". When the 1911 census was taken, his solicitor father had died and he was living with his mother at 32 Park Avenue, Ilkeston. He was employed as a solicitor's articled clerk.

By the time he joined the Royal Naval Reserve on 26th February 1915, he had qualified as a solicitor. Serving first as an ordinary seaman, he was sent to the Signal School at Crystal Palace but was soon awarded a commission as Sub-Lieutenant and drafted to the Howe Battalion Royal Naval Division on 31st May 1915 for service in the Mesopotamian campaign. His record is not clear as to whether he actually served in Iraq, but if so he would have seen the siege of Kut and the battle of Ctesiphon in late 1915. By 18th September 1916, presumably now fighting in France he was marked as sick with influenza and transferred to No 7 Stationary Hospital Boulogne. His record states that he left for England on sick leave 29th September 1916.

Obviously he had a slow recovery, as it was not until 29th May 1917 that he was drafted back to the BEF in Belgium as a musketry instructor. On 6th June he rejoined the Howe Battalion and was appointed a company commander and acting Lieutenant as of 17th June, being promoted to temporary Lieutenant on 23rd October 1917.

Francis was wounded in the arm during the night of 25th October 1917. His chaplain wrote that he "still carried on and proceeded in front of his men to investigate how things were faring. Finding that his steel helmet was interfering with the working of his compass, he discarded it altogether and so fell victim to a sniper, who shot him in the head". Killed in action 26th October 1917, Francis is buried in the Tyne Cot Cemetery near Passchendaele in Belgium.

Francis was also commemorated by Ilkeston's Rutland Masonic Lodge (which he joined in 1914 and in which he rose to the degree of Master Mason) by the planting of a tree at Rutland Sports Park in November 2014.

Varlet Farm

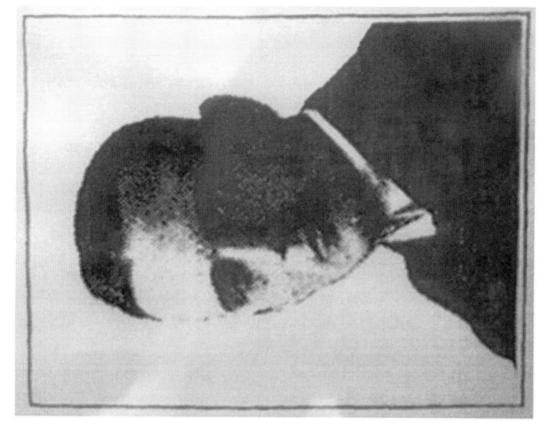

Francis Leonard Hunter Jackson, local Solicitor who fought with the Royal Naval Division and was killed attacking Varlet Farm near Ypres. He had removed his helmet as it was interfering with his compass and was shot in the head.

Grant Shaw

The grave of Herbert Straw in Villers Station Cemetery. A former member of the Army Cyclist Corps, he transferred to the Royal Engineers and was involved in dangerous work with poison gas.

Chapter Six

1918

Submarine lost with all hands - More sailors in the trenches - Flyer shot down - Conspicuous gallantry - Collision in the Irish Sea - Invalided home - The sinking of HMS Britannia - The end of the War?

Frederick Walker,
HM Submarine *K4*, 31st January 1918

A Leading Telegraphist on H.M. Submarine *K4*, Frederick was the son of Robert and Agnes Walker of Dale Abbey. It has not been possible to establish more about his family from the census records.

HMS *K4* was a British K class submarine built by Vickers in Barrow-in-Furness. She was laid down on 28 June 1915 and commissioned on 1 January 1917. The K series were not lucky boats. On 17 November 1917, *K4* collided with sister ship *K1* during an accident off the Danish coast. The crew of *K1* were rescued before their boat sank.

Frederick's boat *K4* was lost on 31 January 1918 during night time fleet exercises. While attempting to avoid a collision with sister boat *K3*, she became the victim of collisions with *K6* and *K7*. She was lost with all hands.

Frederick was 26, and his body was not recovered. He is commemorated on the Plymouth Royal Naval Memorial.

John Mangan
Able Seaman RNVR, 24th March 1918

John's service record from the Royal Naval Volunteer Reserve has fortunately survived.

Born at Ilkeston Junction on 12th June 1898, John's parents were hosiery worker Michael (born in Ireland) and Nottinghamshire born Sarah. He was five feet eight inches high with blue-grey eyes and brown hair and a 'fresh complexion'. His service record states he was a Roman Catholic.

John found work locally as a framework knitter and entered into Naval service in February 1917, aged 18. He was drafted into the BEF on 26th June and joined the sailors of the Hood Battalion fighting in the trenches of the Western Front on 22nd July. He was promoted to Able Seaman the day after. He was reported to have been wounded on 27th October 1917 but rejoined his unit exactly a month later.

Wounded again on 27th February 1918, he rejoined his unit on 21st March.

John Harold Shooter MC

Cossall War Memorial showing the
names of Hezekiah Scattergood
and John Mangan

Edward Lloyd's unmarked grave
in Park Cemetery, Ilkeston

Albert Edward Fairbarnes is
also buried in Park Cemetery

However, only three days later he was reported missing. His family were informed on 20th April. Reports came in that he had been wounded again and captured by the enemy. On 24th September his identity disc and paybook were received from a Saxon Field Hospital, indicating that he had died. On 16th November 1918 he was officially declared to have been killed in action on 24th March and his personal effects were sent to his father as next of kin on 22nd December 1918.

John was buried by the Germans in a plot with other prisoners of war at Cambrai East Military Cemetery. He was 19 years old. He is remembered on the Cossall War memorial.

John Harold Shooter MC,
RAF, 10th April 1918

John was born in 1891, the fourth son of George and Mary Shooter of Wilmot Street, Ilkeston. A choir boy and later Sunday School teacher at Christ Church, Cotmanhay, he attended Heanor Technical School and worked for a while as a clerk at Cossall Colliery. Deciding he would rather be a teacher, he worked for a year teaching at St Mary's School in Ilkeston and after passing a 'scholarship examination' went to St John's Training College at Battersea for a further two years. He appears on the 1911 census as one of 139 resident students there.

He took up a teaching post in Sheffield for a further two years and volunteered for the army in November 1914 as a physical training teacher. After training at Aldershot, he served on the army gymnastic staff in various camps in England before being gazetted a Second Lieutenant with the 2/5 York and Lancaster Regiment. On June 13th 1915 he married Clarice Shelton from Cotmanhay.

John was sent to France on May 10th 1917 and was awarded the Military Cross in July, an award he received directly from King George V at Buckingham Palace.

His citation says that he "showed conspicuous gallantry and devotion to duty in carrying out a daylight patrol to clear up an obscure situation. Accompanied by a private, he showed most exceptional skill and daring in proceeding over unknown and difficult ground in order to ascertain the enemy's forward positions. They returned with very valuable information, having attacked an enemy post and dispersed its garrison, one of whom was shot by the private. Their courage and intelligence proved of the greatest assistance in locating the enemy".

The day after receiving his MC, John was back in France, but returned to England in January having transferred to the Royal Flying Corps. After a short training course, he returned to France and qualified for his Observer's wings with 35 Squadron on 3rd April, two days after the RFC and the Royal Naval Air Service had been combined to form the RAF. He wrote to his mother of his excitement at having flown over the German lines.

By the time his mother received this letter, he was dead. Only a week later, Second Lieutenant Shooter was shot and killed while flying as the observer in an Armstrong Whitworth FK8 (a two seater bi-plane) flown by 2nd Lieutenant McGregor, who was himself unhurt when the FK8 was shot down after combat with enemy aircraft near Merville Bois just before 11am on 10th April 1918.

The Ilkeston Pioneer said that he was "very well known and highly respected". John is buried in Longueau British Cemetery on the outskirts of Amiens, France.

Samuel Kidger
8th Cameronians (Scottish Rifles), 29th July 1918

The Ilkeston Pioneer of 13th September 1918 carried the following report :

"We regret to have to announce that Mrs Kidger, of 92 Station-road, Ilkeston received news on the 27th ultimo of the death of her husband Rifleman Sam Kidger of the [8th Cameronians (Scottish Rifles)], who was killed in action in France on July 29th. When Rifleman Kidger was called to the colours on November 16th 1915, he had worked for Messrs J B Lewis & Sons, Ilkeston Junction for 24 years, as a Cotton's patent hand. He was well known as a cricketer, usually playing with Lewis's, and was greatly respected by all who were acquainted by him. He was 39 years of age, and a son of Mr Wm. Kidger of 73 Station-road. After training at Marton, Middlesbrough and Marske-by-the-Sea, he came home for his draft leave from March 12th to 17th 1916, and was then ordered to Egypt. He left France on board the 'Transylvania' which was torpedoed on May 4th. Two Ilkeston lads lost their lives, and Kidger had a narrow escape of sharing the same fate" [...]

"Shortly afterwards, Rifleman Kidger was sent to Egypt, where he visited Cairo then passed on to Palestine, taking part in the attacks on Gaza and Jerusalem. He again returned to France on the 19th April last, in which country he has laid down his life in the great struggle. The last letter received from him by his wife was dated July 21st, in which he stated that she was not to bother if she did not hear as usual, as he was always moving. His letters were always of a cheerful character, and he was buoyed up with the thoughts of coming home again. He was always longing for the war to end, so that all the boys could come back to the dear ones they had left behind. Great sympathy has been expressed with his widow, who by his death has lost a kind and affectionate husband".

Samuel Kidger was born in Shepshed in 1879 to William and Elizabeth (known as 'Lizzie'). His father was a framework knitter. In 1891 they were living in Kirkby in Ashfield and by 1901 had moved to 61 Station Road Ilkeston where Sam and his father were both described as framework knitters, although they both now worked in a hosiery factory. In the 1911 census he is described as a 'hosiery worker machinist'. Sam was still unmarried, and did not 'tie the knot' with Harriett Beardsley until the summer of 1915.

He joined the Northumberland Fusiliers and was later transferred to the Cameronians (Scottish Rifles). Unfortunately his service record has not survived. Sam was killed on 29th July 1918 aged 39.

Records held by the regiment show that in the last week of July 1918 the 8th Scottish Rifles were among the British regiments who co-operated with the French in the Marne offensive, which proved to be the beginning of victory for the Allies. On July 18th the French began to move forward on a 27-mile front and two days later the Germans were forced to re-cross the river

Marne. On July 23rd there was fierce fighting throughout the sector and 8th Scottish Rifles suffered casualties in what one man calls "the Soissons battle when we were supporting the French". Records of the action are as follows :

"On July 23rd we had just arrived at our position on the Marne front and had dug in. A shell came over about 10 yards away from me and killed or wounded about a dozen men. This was about 7am". For the next six days little progress seems to have been made and on July 29th another hotly contested action took place. "We were advancing at a village near Soissons but were held up by machine gun fire. Some men got into some high growing corn and have not been heard of since. My company dug in".

"We were attacking near Soissons and had men killed by machine gun bullets in the open. We had to retire at 4.30pm and the dead were left. We recovered the ground 2 or 3 days".

In such a desperate struggle as this, men have little opportunity to note or record the fate of their comrades. Sam's sister made extended enquiries even into 1920 to try to establish the location of his body and there are many letters from various official authorities in response to her letters to them. The family have always believed that he was one of the men who was attacking through the high growing corn. A letter dated 29th May 1919 from the Director of Graves Registration, War Office, St James Square, London reads as follows:

"Dear Madam, In reply to your letter of 19th May 1919 I regret that I can only repeat my letter of 28th January 1919 in which I stated that Private S Kidger is reported to be buried in the vicinity of Beugneux on the left side of wood to Servenay SSE of Soissons. You may rest assured that if when my officers are working in this area they are able to locate the grave so that it can be registered in this office, I will at once write to you again, but until this has been done it is impossible for a photograph to be taken. Signed for Major General Director G.C.R.& E."

We understand nothing more was heard and Sam is listed as missing with no known grave. His name is on the war memorials at Ilkeston and at Soissons. His name is also recorded in the book of fatalities in the Regimental Museum of the Cameronians in Edinburgh Castle.

William Ernest Hollis,
RNVR, SS *Burutu*, 3rd October 1918

William was born at Cotmanhay on 17th October, 1888. He may have been known by his second name of 'Ernest'. His parents were John, a Lace Maker and Eliza Jane, who had been born in Wiltshire. By the 1911 census they were living at 187a Nottingham Road, Ilkeston and William was a moulder in the Iron Foundry at Stanton Ironworks. He married Martha Beardsley in early 1914.

On 27th September 1917 he was accepted into the RNVR and spent some time on shore establishments before being sent out to West Africa to join a merchant steamship, the Elder Dempster Lines SS *Burutu* at the end of July 1918. The 3,863 ton *Burutu*, which was 'defensively armed', had been attacked and damaged by a German U-boat off Liberia, West Africa in April while returning home and was undergoing an emergency refit at Freetown, Sierra Leone. On arrival, Hollis wrote to Martha that he had 'a beautiful passage out' and was hoping to be home almost as soon as the letter.

On the way back to Liverpool, *Burutu* entered the Irish Sea in the midst of a gale and heavy seas. Somehow in the early hours of 3rd October 1918 off the coast of South Wales the stern of the much larger liner SS *City of Calcutta* struck the ship on the port side and 'a huge rent was made in the plates of the *Burutu*, and the vessel went down in ten minutes' according to the Ilkeston Pioneer.

Reports said that there had been 'perfect discipline' aboard and that the suddenness of the disaster - while many aboard were asleep - and the hostile conditions made rescue difficult. 42 escaped, but one of the lifeboats capsized in the heavy seas. About 160 perished, including Ordinary Seaman William Ernest Hollis. He was 29 and as his body was never recovered he is remembered on the Plymouth Naval Memorial.

James Frederick Straw MM and bar
1/5 Sherwood Foresters, 24th October 1918

James was born in Awsworth in early 1894. By 1901 his father Jacob, mother Mary and five siblings were living in Holy Trinity Parish in Ilkeston. It has not been possible to track him down on the 1911 census, but we do know that he married Lily Royle, a spinster at Babbington Chapel on Christmas Day 1914. Their son Ralph James was born on 7th January 1916.

On 7th April 1915 James joined the 3/5 Sherwood Foresters as a private. Landing in France on 9th February 1917, in September he was promoted to unpaid Lance Corporal after being transferred to 1/5 Sherwood Foresters. Promotion followed rapidly thereafter, with him being confirmed as a sergeant by December of that year.

James was awarded the Military Medal for gallantry and devotion to duty during an attack on German trenches near Le Hamel (Le Touret) on 20th August 1918 and won a bar to his MM (a second Military Medal in effect) during an attack at St Quentin on 29th September 1918.

News of the bar to his MM may not have reached him before he was seriously wounded and sent to hospital at Rouen. James died of his wounds on 24th October 1918. He is buried in St. Sever Cemetery Extension, Rouen, Normandy.

Albert Edward Fairbarnes
Hampshire Regiment, 6th November 1918

Albert was born in Balderton, Nottinghamshire in June 1883. The 1911 Census finds him boarding with the Brownson household at 12 Crompton Street, Hallam Fields. He was employed as a labourer at the Stanton Ironworks and was unmarried.

He joined the army at Ilkeston on 16th November 1915 and was originally posted to the King's Royal Rifle Corps. It is not clear from his pension records how much of his period with the KRRC was spent serving abroad. On 23rd February 1917 he was transferred to the Hampshire Regiment and at this time was serving in France.

On 23rd March 1917 Albert reported sick, complaining of exhaustion and pains in his legs. Diabetes was suspected. Albert was sent home on 6th April and admitted to the War Hospital at Bradford.

A medical report of May 12th 1917 confirmed the diagnosis of diabetes which, while not caused by his service in the army had been aggravated by serving in the trenches. It found him "weak, feeble and emaciated, has a slow pulse and occasional attacks of faintness," and said that the slightest variation in his diet resulted in him passing large quantities of sugar. Two days later, the Registrar confirmed the Doctor's report and his recommendation that Albert be discharged from the army as permanently unfit for further service, with a note that out-patient treatment would be required.

His time in the army duly ended on 4th June 1917 and Albert was sent home to his mother Susan at 35 Albany Street, Ilkeston. Albert's case was reviewed again on 11th September 1918 and he was found still to have 'total incapacity' and be completely unfit for further service. Still unwell, Albert died on 6th November 1918. He was 35 years old and was buried in Ilkeston's Park Cemetery.

His CWGC headstone bears an inscription from his family : "God moves in a mysterious way".

Edward Clarence Hall
HMS *Britannia*, 9th November 1918

Edward Clarence Hall was born in Ilkeston on 31st July 1896. By the time of the 1901 census, his father Henry had died. His mother remarried in about 1903, changing surname to Grimble.

Edward lived with his mother Sarah Ann, step-father and siblings at 79 Crompton Street, Hallam Fields and they were soon joined by younger step-brothers and sisters. By 1911, aged 14, Edward was working with his step-father and brother at Stanton Ironworks as a general labourer.

Joining the Royal Marine Light Infantry, Edward served as a private on HMS *Britannia*, a pre-dreadnought battleship which had entered service in 1904. Unfortunately she was rendered almost obsolete only three months later when the revolutionary HMS *Dreadnought* was launched, and spent much of WW1 protecting 'dreadnoughts' by looking out for mines, sometimes being deliberately put in harm's way to save the more valuable new ships.

Tyne Cot, near Passendale (Passchendaele), Belgium is a cemetery and a memorial. 11,950 allied and four German soldiers are buried here. The wall also records nearly 35,000 missing in Belgium from August 1917 to the end of the War. Tyne Cot is the largest CWGC cemetery in the world in terms of the number buried here.

94

On the morning of 9th November 1918, *Britannia* was in the western entrance to the Straits of Gibraltar when she was torpedoed off Cape Trafalgar by the German submarine *U-50*. *Britannia* stayed afloat for more than two hours after being hit, allowing most of the crew to be taken off.

Most of the men who were lost were killed by toxic smoke from burning cordite; 50 men died and 80 were injured. In total, 712 of the crew were saved - Edward was not one of them.

Sunk only two days before the Armistice was signed on 11 November 1918, *Britannia* was the last major Royal Navy ship to be lost during World War I. Edward's body was never recovered, and he is remembered on the Portsmouth Naval Memorial.

Edward Lloyd,
12th Sherwood Foresters, 24th November 1918

Edward was born in 1892 in Cotmanhay. His parents were Humphrey and Alvina Lloyd and by 1911 the family had moved to Shirebrook, where both father and son worked as coal hewers in a colliery.

The family moved back to Ilkeston and Edward volunteered for the colours, joining the 12th Sherwood Foresters on 2nd November 1914. His army service record says that he was 5'7" with brown hair and eyes and a fair complexion, and his religion was marked as 'Church of England'.

Serving first in England, he embarked on the SS *Empress Queen* from Southampton on 28th August 1915, arriving at Le Havre the following day.

On 27th November 1915 he married Florence Jane Parry at Awsworth Parish Church. She was 17 years old and expecting their child, Samuel Edward Humphrey Lloyd who was born on 11th May 1916. His mother died the following day, her cause of death stated as being childbirth and complications from her pregnancy.

Baby Samuel, who was being cared for by his father's parents at 15 Nesfield Terrace, Ilkeston died on 24th November, aged just over six months. His cause of death was certified as pulmonary tuberculosis.

On 21st June 1917 Edward suffered multiple gunshot wounds to the right thigh and leg and was sent to a casualty clearing station and then to a field hospital in Camiers, near Etaples, France. On 1st July 1917 he was sent back to England on the hospital ship *Brighton* and was treated at a General Hospital in Manchester.

On 13th July he began to cough, and was diagnosed with pulmonary tuberculosis. A Medical Board discussed his case on 24th September, and the army discharged him as physically unfit and 'totally disabled' on 16th October 1917. He was awarded the 'Silver War Badge' as a war wounded ex-serviceman.

HMS Britannia, torpedoed 9th November 1918. Royal Marine Private Edward Clarence Hall died.

HM Submarine K4, which sank on 31st January 1918 killing Leading Telegraphist Frederick Walker.

Sent for treatment in a sanatorium, he never recovered and died on 12th April 1918 at home with his mother. He was 26. Edward is buried in an unmarked grave at Plot 2238 Park Cemetery Ilkeston, the same grave as his younger brother Arthur and father Humphrey.

Edward had been sent to France at the end of August 1915, married in November 1915, lost his father in January 1916, his wife in May 1916 and his 17 year old brother Arthur and son Samuel within eleven days of each other in November 1916.

Private Edward Lloyd is commemorated on the Park Cemetery War Memorial and on Ilkeston Cenotaph.

Grant Shaw

What's left behind ... when local people reoccupied the battle areas they made use of whatever materials were available to rebuild. This stream in the Somme area is still lined with German shell cases, a century later.

Cecil Baker (right) poses for a souvenir photo in front of the Pyramids in Egypt.

'Nottingham Bakers in France' - A card sent from the 99th Field Bakery.
Is Ted Duro one of these men?

Chapter Seven

AFTER

Some of those who came back

John Cecil Johnson
Lancashire Fusiliers

John was born in Stanley (some records say West Hallam) on 9th January 1896. By 1901 father William, mother Bertha and growing family were living at 25 Thorpe Street, Cotmanhay. William was a miner. By 1911 the family were at 4 Trinity Street, with nine children in total including one year old twins Ernest and William. John, at 15, was a butcher's assistant.

On 19th January 1915 John volunteered for the Corps of Hussars and had a month's training at Scarborough. His service record says he was of 'dark complexion' with grey eyes and dark hair, standing five feet seven and a half inches tall, more than average in those days.

Perhaps cavalry life did not suit him as he was transferred to the Lancashire Fusiliers in July. On 23rd August 1915 his record says he entered the 'Mediterranean theatre' of the war, which we know meant initially Gallipoli. He stayed in this theatre of the war until mid-1916 when he was sent to France. Unfortunately, although his service record has survived, it is heavily water damaged from the Blitz so we have no detail about exactly where he served. However, the Ilkeston Pioneer tells us he was in the 'Signal section' and his records show he had a clean disciplinary record.

John was promoted to unpaid Lance Corporal on 6th February 1918, and this rank was confirmed on 10th April. However by that time he had other things to worry about. On 5th April he was seriously injured by shrapnel in the left side and shoulder. He was operated on in France and sent back to 'Blighty', arriving on 10th April at the 1st South General Hospital in King's Heath, Birmingham where he was visited by his parents. He showed them his signaller's watch, the case of which had been ripped open by a piece of shrapnel and may well have saved his life.

The Pioneer also reported on 26th April that his brother Driver Ferdinand Johnson was also in hospital (in Woolwich) suffering 'from illness, believed to be the result of having been wounded three times'.

John did not have a speedy recovery and seems to have been disabled to some degree for the rest of his life. He was not properly discharged by the hospital in Birmingham until 3rd September 1919, when a board recommended that he be discharged from the army and reported his 'earning capacity' as only 30% of normal. As a wounded ex-serviceman he was awarded the Silver War Badge but had to wait until January 1920 to get it.

Sadly, there is no happy ending. His pension records state that John died on 25th May 1923 aged only 27.

Lily Barker

Arthur's brother Jack (John Thomas) Wright, seen recovering in his 'hospital blues' uniform. After developing trench foot, he was later gassed and never fully recovered, dying of heart failure and bronchitis in 1925.

Lily Barker

George Arthur Wright, known as 'Arthur' survived the war and worked for many years as a Managing Clerk at John Ormond Solicitors in Ilkeston. He was elected a Borough Councillor and served as Mayor of Ilkeston in 1950.

John Thomas ('Jack') Wright
Notts & Derby Regiment (Sherwood Foresters)

Jack was born in 1888, the second surviving child of thirteen. His parents were Joseph and Martha; Joe owned a hairdressing business on South Street and later on the Market Place at Ilkeston. His family lived 'over the shop', which was extended around the corner in the early 1900's when Wharncliffe Road was created.

Jack worked in a glove factory locally and joined the Sherwood Foresters on 4th April 1915. He was a bugler and acted as a stretcher bearer. Unfortunately his service record has not survived but we know that he spent a period in hospital due to trench foot and suffered serious consequences from being gassed later in the war. A family story says that out of eight men manning a gun he was the only one who survived and his medal record says that he was discharged from the army on 31st August 1917. Jack had met Edith Walker, whose parents kept the 'Prince of Wales' Pub, before he went off to war and they married in May 1919.

He spent a long time 'invalided' although he was able to undertake some work and always took his children John Thomas and Lily to see their grandparents on a Sunday. After a long period of rehabilitation, Jack eventually found employment as a labourer at Stanton Ironworks.

After a long wait, he was awarded a pension in mid-1925. Sadly, things soon took a turn for the worse and he died at home at 77 Lord Haddon Road on 6th December 1925 of bronchitis and heart failure. He was 37. Edith gave birth to a second daughter, June Mary not long after his death. She never remarried and died in 1950 aged 64. Jack is buried in Park Cemetery.

George Bertram Aldred
Able Seaman, RNVR

While searching for details of the slightly elusive Reuben Shaw (q.v.) his service record from the National Archives came attached to that of George, whose service number precedes Reuben's (Z/5645 and Z/5646). They both enlisted in the Royal Navy Volunteer Reserve on 21st November 1916 and it is therefore quite possible that they were pals.

George was born on 27th September 1897 and in the 1901 census was living on Chaucer Street with mother Elizabeth Ann and father George, a lace maker. By 1911 they had moved to 220 Nottingham Road and Elizabeth was now a 'news vendor', her eldest son George (13) and second son Frederick (11) being 'news boys'.

George is described as a 'tram driver' on his enlistment record and he served throughout the rest of the war, although his record does not go into detail as to where. He was promoted Able Seaman in February 1918 and apparently came through the war without serious injury. He was demobbed on 28th February 1919 and married Elsie Leighton not long after.

George died in December 1977 aged 80.

Grant Shaw

The Soissons Memorial commemorates almost 4,000 of the United Kingdom forces who died during the Battles of the Aisne and the Marne in 1918 and who have no known grave. Sam Kidger is one of them.

Anne Hadfield

Charles Henry (Charlie) Carpenter

102

Cecil John Baker
Royal Garrison Artillery

Cecil was born in December 1886. His father William was a blacksmith and in 1901 he, parents and six siblings were living at 40 Albert Street. He was employed as a 'pawnbroker's errand boy' at age 14. By 1911 his widowed mother Rebecca had only three sons living at home, Cecil being by now a 'Gas Inspector' for Ilkeston Corporation. In 1914 he married Hannah Beardsley. Their son Cecil Beardsley Baker was born in 1915.

Unfortunately, Cecil's service record seems not to have survived, but his medal record tells us he joined the Royal Garrison Artillery with the rank of Gunner.

He told his son many years later that he had fought the Austrians at Caporetto in what is now Slovenia. This battle, fought in October/November 1917 was a German/Austrian victory against the Italians, who were forced to retreat quickly but fought back with allied help the next year.

Although we do know there were British units at the Battle of Vittorio Veneto next year, it has not been possible to establish whether he would actually have fought at Caporetto or on the retreat which followed. However, his papers include a handwritten copy of a letter apparently from the Royal Italian Army confirming that he was entitled to wear an Italian military medal. This is dated before the battle and he said that due to the speed of the retreat he never had time to collect the decoration.

After fighting with the Italians Cecil was posted to the Eastern Mediterranean, landing in Egypt (where he had his photograph taken riding a camel in front of the pyramids) and then to Jerusalem. He said that he walked from Gaza to Damascus on foot, with the artillery pieces being pulled by camels in the desert. Damascus fell at the end of the campaign, on 1st October 1918 and the Ottoman Empire signed an armistice on 30th October 1918.

Cecil told his son that 'having been involved in the fastest retreat in military history from Caporetto' he went on to join 'the fastest advance, from Suez to Damascus'.

After the war Cecil went back to live in Ilkeston with his family at 28 Station Road. He worked at the Royal Ordnance Factory at Chilwell and was a keen bell ringer at St. Mary's, Ilkeston. Cecil died in April 1953 aged 66.

Charles Henry Carpenter
1st Battalion, Sherwood Foresters

Charlie, as he was known, was born in 1890 and in the 1901 census he is living with his widowed father Henry (his mother Elizabeth having died between 1896 and 1901) who was a stone quarry man and five of his siblings at 66 Hempshill Lane, Bulwell. We have not been able to locate Charlie on the 1911 census, which may mean that he was already a professional soldier.

Anne Hadfield

"We've done our bit and ready for more". Charlie Carpenter and comrades, probably all from 1st Sherwood Foresters. Charlie was a professional soldier from Awsworth who served in India before the War and survived the conflict.

At the outbreak of war, Charlie was serving with the 1st Battalion the Sherwood Foresters in Bombay (Mumbai) India, which he had joined as a drummer. Hastily summoned back to Europe on the outbreak of war, they embarked on the *SS Tongwa* from Bombay on 2nd September 1914 and arrived at Plymouth on 2nd October. After some training near Winchester, they took a troop ship a month later from Southampton and landed in France on 5th November 1914.

Family stories say that he took part in the famous 'Christmas Truce' of 1914.

His battalion celebrated Christmas a day early and helped demolish some of the 1,100 plum puddings which had been sent to the troops by the City and County of Nottingham in their billets at 'Red Barn' before going back to the front line. They were indeed in the trenches at Richebourg on 25th December and the battalion's War Diary records that they relieved the 2nd East Lancashire Regiment in the front line and :

"Relief completed. This was the quickest relief we have yet had, due to entire lack of fire and to severe frost on night of 24th/25th. An informal armistice was arranged between some of Germans opposite 'A' lines and 2nd East Lancs and during this time both sides collected the dead in front of the trenches".

We can't confirm whether Charlie participated in the famous 'fraternisation' with the enemy that Christmas Day but at least we know he *was* in the vicinity. Unfortunately we have no more detail about his career as his service record has not survived. Happily, he did.

Charlie married Mary Ann Cadman in Autumn 1915 and lived at 63 Park Hill, Awsworth after the War. He died in December 1963 aged 73.

Hubert Chester Spiby
1/5th Sherwood Foresters

Hubert, known as 'Bert' was born on 19th May 1892 in Ilkeston. He was the son of Arthur Clement Spiby and his wife Alice. Arthur was the gardener who laid out Victoria Park and was for 30 years its superintendent. His family lived at 34 Bristol Road, opposite the park. Horticulture was the family trade; his grandfather had been head gardener at Sutton Bonington Hall and Bert and his three brothers all held responsible posts as park superintendents or playing fields managers.

As one of the original 'Ilkeston Terriers' Bert was in camp at Hunmanby near Filey when war was declared and was one of those who left Ilkeston amid great ceremony shortly after.

Promoted to Lance Corporal almost immediately, he was with the regiment while billeted in Harpenden, Hertfordshire and landed in France on 2nd March 1915. After this he was promoted to Sergeant, and joined in the 'diversionary' attack on Gommecourt on 1st July 1916, the first day of the Battle of the Somme.

William Everard Henshaw, who survived the war (above) and with his pals before going off to war. He is on the right.

During this action, Bert was shot in the head, the bullet leaving him with a deep depression above his right cheekbone and deafness. While injured, Bert was captured, and spent the rest of the war in prison camps.

"Sergt. H. C. Spiby, who was taken prisoner by the Germans on July 1, 1916, and has returned to his home in Ilkeston, had a miraculous escape from death at the time of his capture.

He was struck by a grenade, and lay 'on the top' close to the German trenches. In order to ease the pain of his wound, he made an effort to rid himself of his equipment, and was at once hit in the head by the bullet of a sniper. When he recovered consciousness, twelve days later, he found himself in a hospital at St. Quentin, and for another month he suffered from partial lockjaw, and was completely deaf.

He was transferred to a hospital at Ohrdruf, [Thuringia, central Germany] and such was the deplorable state of affairs there through lack of attention that in the month of August there were men whose wounds were overrun with white maggots, and daily several men were carried out dead.

He left this hospital on October 12, 1916, and was taken to a prisoners' camp accommodating about 12,000 men, the commandant of which, he declared, was a lace maker in Nottingham. The authorities made strict enquiries as to each man's trade, in order to put him to work. Spiby always described himself as a soldier, and escaped, but one man put himself down as a 'lion tamer', and thought he would be safe. To his mortification, he was sent for work in a menagerie!"

Ilkeston Pioneer, December 6, 1918.

Bert was repatriated at the end of 1918 and eventually discharged from the army on 1st April 1919.

Bert was in charge of Ilkeston's Rutland Recreation Ground from its opening in 1925 until his retirement and became an expert groundsman. He made an appearance in the Derby Daily Telegraph in 1929 which is reprinted later in this book. Bert married twice, to Edith Billingham in 1920 (deceased 1942) and in 1944 to Ada Moorley, who survived him.

He died in 1977, after suffering a stroke aged 84.

Albert Cade MM
RAMC, HMHS *Essequibo* and elsewhere

Albert was the youngest son of William and Mary Ann and was born on 21st September 1897 at Langley. His father worked as a collier at Langley and Shipley Coppice pits. With his five brothers, he attended Clara Mount School and was a member of the local church, winning prizes for good attendance.

Albert Cade MM

Albert served in the Royal Army Medical Corps in Malta, Egypt, Canada, France and Belgium
as well as on the Hospital Ship *Essequibo*. He won the Military Medal while in France.
(Left) Dressed up as a sailor from the *Essequibo* (Right) with a mate in Egypt in 1915/16

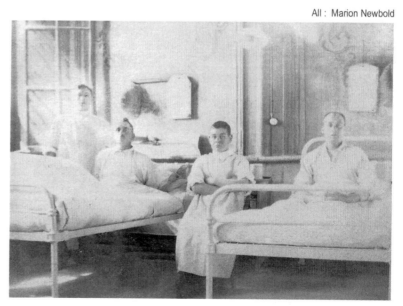

(Right) On his ward in Egypt (Albert is on the left) in a temperature of 120 degrees in the shade
(Left) with wife Connie on holiday in Jersey in later life

Leaving school at 13, Albert worked as a pony driver underground. He joined the St John Ambulance Brigade and by 1911 the family had moved to 39 Awsworth Road, Ilkeston where they had a grocery shop.

Albert joined the Royal Army Medical Corps in May 1915, serving in Malta in 1915, Egypt 1915-1916, Canada in 1917 and France and Belgium in 1918. Whilst in Egypt he was photographed on his hospital ward "with AWA patients taken in a temperature of 120 degrees in the shade" (AWA indicates respiratory or airway problems).

In July 1916 he was confirmed into the Anglican faith by the Bishop of Jerusalem in Cairo. He received his first communion at the Citadel Chapel in Cairo in August 1916.

Albert was stationed onboard a Hospital Ship, the *Essequibo* (a requisitioned Royal Mail Line passenger steamer) in early 1917 on a voyage carrying wounded from the eastern Mediterranean back to England. On 15th March she was almost home when off the South-West Irish coast she was fired upon and forced to stop by a German submarine.

U54 was commanded by Kapitanleutnant Baron Volkhard von Bothmer (1882-1948), who had been about to attack the *Essequibo* until he saw that she was a hospital ship.

A boarding party were sent on board and they confirmed *Essequibo*'s status, leaving her unharmed and wishing her a good voyage. In thanks, the ship's crew gave them three cheers. Astonishingly, Albert's photographs of the submarine and the boarding party's boat have survived and we have printed them in this book. *U54* went on to stop and torpedo a French sailing cargo ship, the 2203 ton *Eugene Pergeline* later that day.

In 1918, while serving with the 33rd Division of the BEF on the Western Front, Albert was awarded the Military Medal for 'bravery in the field 19th-27th September'. The 99th Field Ambulance War Diary says that Albert's unit dealt with over 100 wounded whilst under fire and treated 170 gas cases in one day on 24th September. He was presented with his MM as part of the 'Official Celebration of the Treaty of Peace' on 19th July 1919.

His 'character certificate' given on discharge describes him as 'a sober, honest and trustworthy man'. After serving his time during the War, Albert remained in the Army Reserve for a further eight years.

He married Constance ('Connie') Ault in 1925 aged 27 and worked on the railways, being at one time Stationmaster at Shipley Gate Station. Albert retired in 1962 and died in 1979 aged 81.

Allen Straw
Notts & Derby Regiment (Sherwood Foresters)

Allen was born in 1897 in Ilkeston. His parents were James and Sarah Jane (nee Meakin) and in 1901 they and his eight siblings were living at 23 John Street. By 1911 they were living at 28 Bristol Road and the return says that James and Sarah had had twelve children in total. Allen is employed as a 'grocer's errand boy'.

Unfortunately, neither Allen's Service Record nor his Pension Record seem to have survived, but we do know that he was conscripted and joined the Sherwood Foresters on 22nd April 1918 aged 20. Not long after reaching the front he was seriously wounded by shrapnel in the right shoulder and left buttock. His parents received a telegram informing them that he was missing, believed dead.

Their emotions can only be imagined at receiving a second telegram eighteen months later telling them that he was still alive and was now in the Manchester Royal Infirmary with his wounds and what may have been shell shock.

Allen recovered sufficiently to return home to be a miner again - he was finally discharged by the army on 5th September 1919 - but he carried the scars for the rest of his life. He was awarded the Silver War Badge (no. B297570) as a disabled ex-soldier, together with a small pension. He married in August 1930 and had a family.

Allen died in 1972 aged 75.

Edwin Jeffery,
Royal Army Medical Corps

Edwin was born on 19th August, 1897 in Ilkeston. The 1901 census shows him living with father (also Edwin), mother Lydia and four siblings at 21 Prince Street, Cotmanhay. He was educated at Bennerley School, and like his father became a miner.

In 1911 they were living at 1 Prince Street. By 1913 they had moved to 136, Cotmanhay Road and Edwin was working at Woodside Colliery, Shipley. He had four sisters and two brothers with whom he corresponded frequently during the war.

He enlisted on 22nd May 1915 in the Royal Army Medical Corps and was based at the Military Hospital, West Bridgford. He went to Ripon Camp in Yorkshire before being posted to Malta, where he served at St. Elmo Hospital until 12th July 1918, when he was posted to Italy.

Edwin Jeffery

Edwin served in the Royal Army Medical Corps in Malta and Italy.
He died only a few months after returning to his job as a coal miner in 1919.

A portrait of Edwin in his RAMC uniform and
(right) his shaving mirror in its leather case, made by E J Newton of Bath Street, Ilkeston.

All : John and Jenifer Giblin

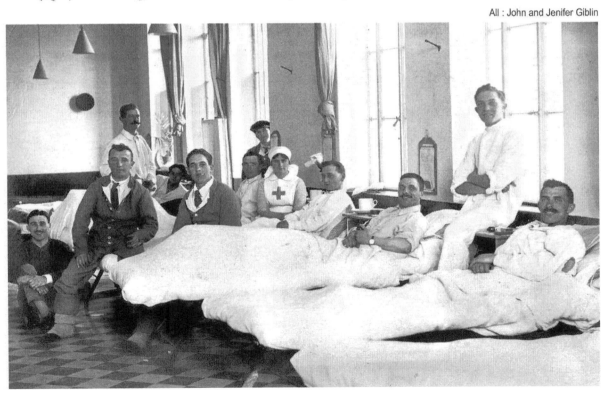

On the ward in Malta with survivors from the torpedoed troop ship *Cameronia* on which Ilkeston's
John Hendy and 209 others died, April 1917. Edwin is standing, right. The servicemen to
the left are wearing 'hospital blues' - service dress but coloured blue with white shirt and red tie.

All : Ken Mather

A fresh faced Jack Mather before going off to war (above, left) and some time later, taken in France while on active service (above, right).

Right : Jack after being wounded and invalided out of the army. He wears his Silver War Badge denoting him as a wounded ex-serviceman.

Jack was born in 1896 and worked at the Woodside Colliery until ill health forced his early retirement in 1939. He died in 1948 aged only 52.

Edwin arrived back in the UK on 23rd January 1919 and was demobbed at the North Camp, Ripon the next day. On returning home he took up his previous occupation as a coal miner, but sadly died on 28th July 1919 following treatment to a boil on his forehead. He was 21.

His family have preserved many items from his war service, some of which we have been very pleased to include in this book.

Jack Mather
Royal Field Artillery

Jack was born in 1896. A miner, he worked for the Shipley Colliery Company before the war. He joined the Royal Field Artillery at their depot in Newcastle Upon Tyne at the start of January 1915, his father Herbert of 30 Awsworth Road Ilkeston being named as 'next of kin' on his record. Ranked throughout his service as a gunner, he landed in France on 18th May 1915.

Jack was wounded on 15th July 1916 and was taken to the army's General Hospital at Camiers. The gunshot wound to his neck was deemed to be 'slight' and he was discharged on 30th July.

A year later in August 1917 he was more severely wounded, being shot in the left cheek and forearm, with 'severe' damage caused to his eye. Admitted to No.1 Australian General Hospital at Rouen, he was eventually sent back to England and spent some time in hospital in Walmer, Kent.

It was obviously a painful and slow recovery, as he was not transferred from hospital to an RFA Reserve Battalion until after a medical board on 28th August 1918. Given an initial pension of 27 shillings and sixpence a month, he was finally formally discharged from the army on 17th January 1919. Jack had his photograph taken wearing his Silver War Badge as a wounded ex-serviceman.

Jack married a girl he had met in London while recuperating and started a family. He went back to Woodside Colliery but was never completely well and had to retire from work due to illness in 1939, aged just 43. Jack died in 1948.

William Everard Henshaw,
7th Sherwood Foresters

William was born in 1898, the son of Amos - a 'house furniture dealer' and Clara. Aged 12, he was still at school when the 1911 census was taken.

He served in the 7th Battalion, Notts & Derby Regiment (Sherwood Foresters) but his records did not survive the Blitz. We know little else about William, except that he survived the war and may have stayed in the army for a time afterwards.

William Ernest Britton

Will Britton as a fresh-faced volunteer and with mates Danny Booth and Bill Bradley

All : Nora Waite and Marion Axford

William Britton (third from left) with members of the Burns Street Baptist Church, 1919.
At least one of his friends wears a silver war badge, indicating a wounded veteran.

Several photographs of him during his army service have been donated to us, including two when he had just joined up, looking very young indeed. One of the later photographs seems to show him as an officer cadet.

William married Gladys Langton in the winter of 1922. He died in the autumn of 1978, aged 80.

William Ernest Britton
Royal Field Artillery

Will was born on 24th September 1896. In 1901 he was living with his parents James and Eliza at 20 Carr Street; his father's occupation is stated as 'assistant Colliery Deputy'. By 1911 the family were living at 32 Eyre's Gardens but sadly without mother Eliza, who had died in 1904. At 14, Will's occupation was stated as 'horse boy underground in mine'. Will's service record has not been found, but his medal record tells us that he joined the Royal Field Artillery early in the war and landed in France on 29th July 1915.

Returning home in 1919, he was given an official welcome by fellow Baptists at the Church of Christ on Burns Street, Ilkeston in March that year. Photographs show him looking rather reflective along with some comrades wearing their silver war badges as wounded ex-servicemen. Will was among those invited to the Ilkeston Corporation's 'Official Celebration of the Treaty of Peace' on the Pimlico Recreation Ground (now Rutland Sports Park) on 19th July 1919 and his invitation has survived. Will married Hilda Allen in June 1920 and rejoined the Royal Artillery in the Second World War. He died aged 75 in 1971.

Nora Waite, his daughter, recalls Will's time in the Great War :

"Dad left his job at Gedling Colliery on 30th June 1914. He was in the army until he returned to Gedling on 3rd June 1918. After his training he was eventually sent to France. He was in the trenches, on or near the front line for many months. Many soldiers were shell-shocked, gassed, badly wounded and killed. Dad was one of the fortunate ones. He told my cousin that all the soldiers had a daily ration of five 'Wild Woodbine' cigarettes which he swapped with five of his friends for a drink of water.

Another story Dad told my cousin was about the night when there was not enough room in the trench for all the men to sleep and Dad volunteered to sleep in the field above. That was the night the Germans dropped mustard gas. The gas sank into the trench but Dad escaped the effect of it being at a higher level. I don't know if the men in the trench died or were ill, my cousin didn't know.

Dad never talked about the war to his four daughters. One of the things we did hear about was Dad's homecoming from the war. The story goes that when Dad eventually arrived from France he was lousy and his father would not let him into the house.

A tin bath was filled with water (warm, I hope). Dad had to strip off in the back yard and wash his hair and have a good bath before he was welcomed into the house. I don't know if the dirty clothes were put into the bath afterwards or if they were put into the dustbin. Dad was only 17 years old when he volunteered and 21 when he came home. We were so well blessed to have such a man for our father."

Here he stands
Tall and proud,
Brave and courageous
And still only a boy.

Handsome and smiling
Curly-haired and bright eyed,
Too young for khaki
He is still only a boy.

Alone and afraid
And far from his home,
No letters from loved ones
Still only a lad.

Bombs and bullets
Cries and moans,
Deafening bombardment
The deathly silence more frightening then noise

Valiantly enduring
Watching comrades fall,
Wallowing in mud
Conquering all.

Still in his khaki but lousy as hell
So glad to be home,
And still only a lad
But deep inside he is a broken man.

Nora Waite

Joseph Stevenson MM
Royal Engineers Special Brigade

Joseph was born in Ilkeston and enlisted there in January 1915, serving with the Royal Field Artillery as a driver and landing in France that August. He transferred to the Royal Engineers Special Brigade (which mostly dealt with the use of poison gas) in July 1916.

In October 1917 he was awarded the Military Medal for rescuing ammunition wagons under constant shellfire at Loos near the French/Belgian border. The citation reads :

Joseph Stevenson, as a new recruit to the Royal Field Artillery (left)
and as a seasoned Pioneer in the Royal Engineers (right)

Joseph Stevenson MM (third from left) on a spot of well-earned leave at the Palace of Versailles, 1918

"For conspicuous bravery on the night of 15th August 1917 between Philosophe and Loos. This man was returning with a party from the line and came to a point on the road where 11 [...] Ammunition Wagons blocked the traffic. The officer in charge of the wagons was dangerously wounded, the sergeant with him was killed and three of the men and one or two of the horses were wounded. Pioneer Stevenson gave most valuable assistance in straightening the teams and he rode one of the horses in the team which was conducted to the gun positions by an officer of the battery. In spite of the confusion then existing and in the face of the enemy's continuous shell fire, Pnr. Stevenson by his coolness and entire disregard of danger assisted in averting what would have been a disastrous situation".

Joseph spent leave in Paris between 5th and 12th February 1918 and had his photograph taken at the Palace of Versailles.

On the night of 30th August 1918 he was injured when he fell into a deep trench in the pitch darkness and was sent to hospital, but rejoined his unit four days later. In 1918 he was sent to hospital twice in total but made it through the war, being demobbed in December 1918 and formally discharged the following month as 20% disabled due to what we would now call combat stress.

Joseph Daniel Ellaby MM
Royal Engineers

Joe was born on 27th March 1895 on French Street, Ilkeston.

An Iron moulder at Stanton Ironworks, Joe served with the Royal Engineers from 1916 to 1919 in France and Belgium and was awarded the Military Medal for bravery in the field. He worked at one time on sound ranging, a method of determining the coordinates of enemy artillery using data obtained from the sound of its guns, mortars or rockets firing. This could also be used to direct artillery fire at a previously identified location.

Joe was promoted to Sergeant within two years and kept a diary during this time. He also left many photos, some of which show scenes of rest and recuperation away from the front and are reprinted here. He also brought back a long strip photograph view 'over the top' marked with geographical features for artillery ranging over the enemy trenches.

After the armistice, Joe remained as part of the clean-up effort, and after he was demobbed he went back to his old job at Stanton Ironworks where he worked on making benzine (a liquid fuel) during the Second World War in Stanton's coke ovens.

Joe lived on Inglefield Road not far from the house which was destroyed in a bombing raid in the Second World War. He married Grace Lester (who had worked in the armaments Factory at Chilwell during the Great War) in 1920 and died in 1971 aged 76.

Joseph Ellaby (right) and mates relaxing at a picnic in France or Belgium.

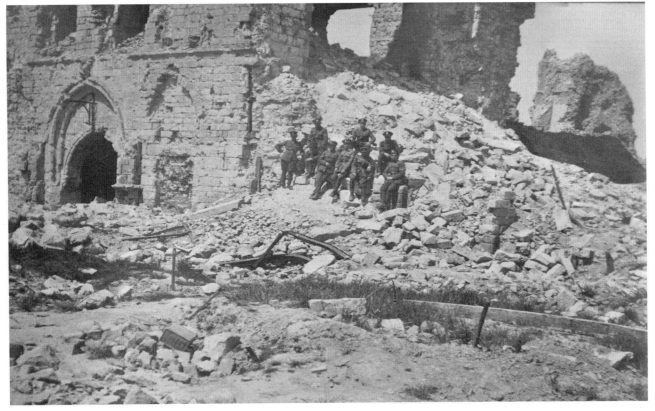

Joseph Ellaby and comrades visiting the ruins of the ancient Cloth Hall and Cathedral in
Ypres, Belgium just after the Armistice.

In the ruined Cathedral at Ypres, Belgium after the Armistice. The whole town, complete with its medieval Cloth Hall and Cathedral was rebuilt after the war.

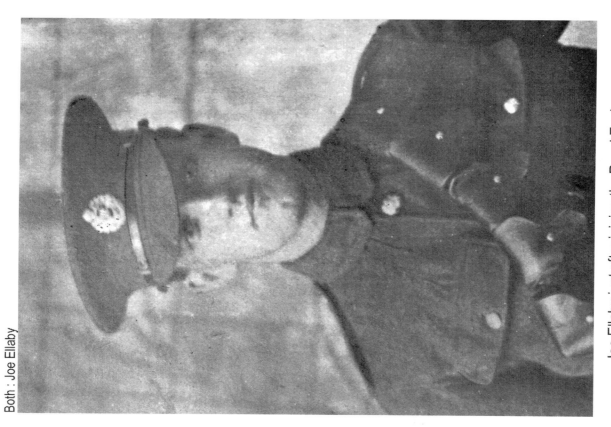

Both : Joe Ellaby

Joe Ellaby just after joining the Royal Engineers

120

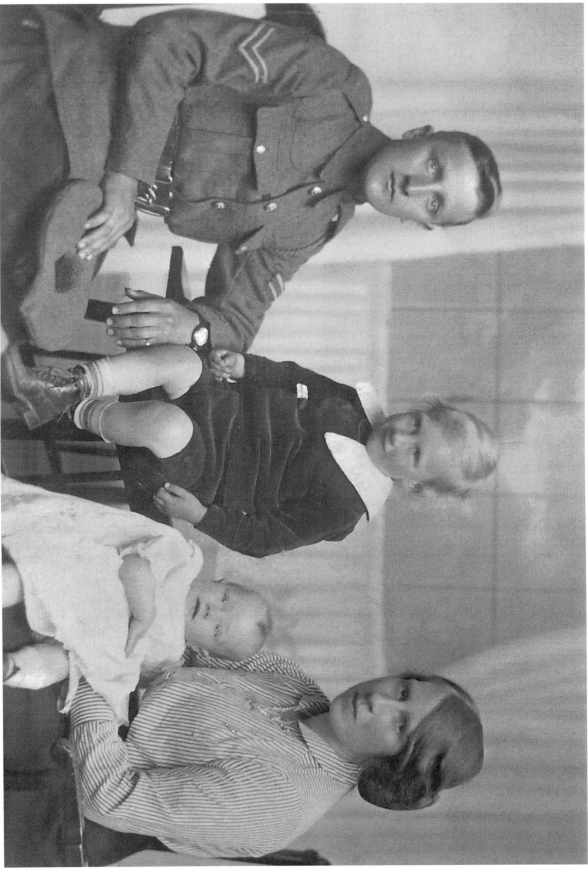

Corporal Enos Langston Saunders later in the war with his young family.
He is wearing his 'Black Watch' uniform, complete with kilt and Tam O'Shanter cap.

Enos Langston Saunders
Army Cyclist Corps and The Black Watch

Enos was born on 23rd September 1892 at Hallam Fields. His parents were Martha and George. He was baptised at St Bartholomew's Church, Hallam Fields on 19th October 1892. The 1911 census shows his occupation as 'Lace Threader'.

Unfortunately his service record is one of the many which have been lost or destroyed, but we know that Enos joined the Army Cyclist Corps early in the War. Transferred to 9th (Service) Battalion of the Royal Highlanders (Black Watch), Enos landed at Boulogne on 8th July 1915.

He may have seen action at the Battle of Loos (September/October 1915), with German gas attacks and then at Pozieres, Flers-Corcelette (Somme 1916) Arras (1917), Langemarck, Pilkem (3rd Ypres) and the second Battle of the Somme as the enemy finally retreated in 1918.

After the War, Enos worked for 57 years at Stanton Ironworks as a pipe moulder and at the Dale Spun Plant. Working until he was 70, he lived in Stapleford and died in June 1969.

William Henry Bestwick
Tank Corps

William was born in early 1891 to Henry and Harriett Bestwick, who ran the family stationers' business which was to be a part of Ilkeston life on the Lower Market Place until the death of his younger brother Nelson in the late 1980's. The 1911 census finds him aged 20 living with his parents and with his occupation stated as 'Assisting in the family business'. In May 1916 he married Edith Toplis.

He was called up in October 1916 and was posted to the Machine Gun Corps in November. Receiving training involving motorised transport, he was posted to 'B' Company of the 6th Battalion in the newly formed Tank Corps in February 1918 and became a tank driver. By August 1918 he was driving a Whippet tank during the Battle of Amiens. The Whippet was a lighter, faster tank than the commonly seen First World War types although it was unsprung and notoriously difficult to steer.

His tank fought in actions on 5th and 6th August 1918 and he came through uninjured. Will reported back home that he had visited a number of hastily abandoned German dugouts and found them 'beautifully furnished with plush chairs and couches, large mirrors, etc' according to the Ilkeston Pioneer.

He was in action again on 23rd August. The Thursday morning following, his father received this letter :

"Dear Mr Bestwick. I am writing to you as a friend of your son Will, he not being with us to-day; yesterday he swent into action with his 'bus', being the driver. Unfortunately everyone was wounded. As far as we can ascertain, none of them was seriously hurt and we all hope Will is not much worse [...] He will be able to look back on yesterday as being a big day for the British Army, and having been one of the participants in a most important battle, which brought us a very large number of prisoners, also the recovery of a large extent of French territory,"

The Pioneer on 6th September reported that Will was back in England and had been visited by his wife and parents, saying also that his tank had become disabled and he had been injured in the legs and left foot by shrapnel while crawling back to the British lines. By 10th November Will was back in Ilkeston General Hospital, being treated for septicaemia as well as his other injuries by GP Dr Tobin. He was allowed home for a few days and by 1st December the Doctor recorded that he was 'slightly improved, ankle stiff'.

Discharged from the hospital in January 1919, he was allowed 28 days' furlough to recover. In February he was transferred to the Army Reserve and finally discharged from the Army on 31st March 1920. Judged to be 30% disabled, he was granted a pension of 12 shillings a week until April 1922, when his army records end.

In one of those fascinating little glimpses which the Army Records sometimes throw up, the list of personal effects shipped back to Will from the French hospital has survived. These were "Handkerchief, pair of gloves, bathing drawers, false teeth". Will duly acknowledged receipt of these important items on 9th April 1919. William Henry Bestwick died at the age of 59 on 26th October 1950. He was survived by his widow, Edith.

George Towndrow Bradley
Sherwood Foresters and Royal Flying Corps

George was born at Stretton near Ashover in 1891 to parents George and Elizabeth. He was baptised at Clay Cross Parish Church in July 1892 and married Annie Mary in June 1914, then living on Albert Street in Ilkeston. Formerly working as a chauffeur/valet, he volunteered for the Notts & Derby Regiment very early in the War and according to his Medal Record 'entered the Field' on 28th February 1915.

Transferring to the Royal Flying Corps in April 1916, he was transferred on into the RAF with the rest of the RFC at its creation on 1st April 1918 and ended the war as a Sergeant, being a colonel's batman for some time. He was finally discharged from the RAF Reserve on 30th April 1920.

After the War, George and Annie had three children. He worked as a lorry driver for Ilkeston Borough Council and died in 1963 aged 71. He is buried in Park Cemetery, Ilkeston.

Colin Greaves

Grant Shaw

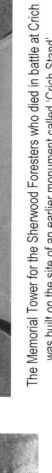

George Towndrow Bradley (right)
in his Royal Flying Corps uniform.

The Memorial Tower for the Sherwood Foresters who died in battle at Crich was built on the site of an earlier monument called 'Crich Stand'. Taking the form of a lighthouse, it was dedicated in 1923 and an annual 'pilgrimage' is still held there on the first Sunday of July.

Chapter Eight

NEWS FROM THE FRONT

Ilkeston Advertiser, August 6th 1915
What life is like at the front

The following very interesting letter, written by Pte Hy. [Henry] Shaw, of the Fifth Sherwoods, has been forwarded to us for publication:

Dear ---

I am just taking this opportunity to let you know how things are going with us out here. In my previous letters I have not been able to tell you much about the interesting side of things, but I have more time. Perhaps this epistle would prove interesting to the folks at home if published in a local paper. If you think so, I have no objection.

Well, our first experience under fire was not at all pleasant. We started from our rest billets at dusk and arrived at the Dumping Station at dark. My company were to be in reserve in a barn just behind the trenches, and while here had to take supplies to the trenches at nights. We arrived and staked our claims out in the barn, and were told to turn out for fatigue. Our work this time was to take some fuel and empty biscuit tins up to the line. We started off and were swinging along fine until something went zipp! In less that 1 sec. every man was flat and doing his best to make himself invisible. That was the first shot.

We got up and continued on our way and came into an open flat piece of ground, which afterwards proved to be very dangerous. It was here that we started seeing things. As soon as a flare went up from the trenches we had orders to drop flat. The mud was inches deep, and it was raining at the time, but things like that did not affect us. We had orders at this time to make no noise, and one of our fellows, who was carrying two empty biscuit tins, turned round to his partner and told him to be quiet, and almost at the same minute fell into a shell hole with his tins. He made enough noise to shake the earth. It is very funny to think about it now, but it made us all very nervous at the time. Well, we went on, and somehow our guide had missed the communication trench that led to the firing trench, and as a result we went right up to the back of the trenches and got straight in. it is a good thing that we were all blissfully unconscious of the fact, or I am afraid we should have felt a bit nervous. That night's work, although it would be quite a commonplace incident now, will always be remembered by us all. We got safely back to our barn, and were all thankful.

While in reserve in this place we had orders not to leave the barn in daylight and to make no smoke by day and no light by night as it was in full view of the lines, and if the enemy thought there were troops in it we should soon have been shelled out. Well, the next day passed without event, but at night we were at it again. This time we were told off to help some engineers make a new firing trench. The road to the trench was very dangerous, and as we were carrying boxes on poles it proved to be more so. However, we got there safely after a series of dashes and were told our work by the R.E.'s. the enemy had seen that we had started this trench and consequently kept on sending star shells up, and at the same time opening rapid fire. This hampered us a lot, and at the finish of our work made it very dangerous to attempt to get back.

Finally it was arranged for us to go in separate parties of about ten. The first party had two men wounded and the others made a dash. At last it came to our turn, but at this time the firing had got worse. So we had to go a roundabout way by the trenches to another communication trench. We got to the end of this trench, and as it was pitch dark and the trench sides were slippy and deep it was difficult to get out of it. Those that got out first had to lay on top and pull the others out. The bullets were whistling round us, still we were not all out, but at last word came up that everyone was ready and we got safely back. It was a miracle that no one was hit on that night in our party.

The following night my platoon was told off to garrison the trench we had made the night before, and accordingly got into our marching order. All went well until we got into the wrong trench. We were in line, and as we got

The memorials

People sought to come to terms with their personal grief and the enormity of the sacrifice made in the Great War by an unprecedented number of memorials of all kinds.

Ilkeston's sombre Cenotaph being unveiled. It was designed by local architect Harry Tatham Sudbury.

The Cenotaph today. Centre of the annual Act of Remembrance, it is difficult to imagine the Market Place without it.

West Hallam's War Memorial, topped by a statue of two Vickers Gunners in marble. It commemorates those who served and those who fell. The relocated Mapperley Collieries War memorial now adjoins it. This is the dedication in the presence of the Bishop of Derby on 12th August 1921.

farther the worse the mud became, until at last it was above our knees. The heavy equipment on our backs and our rifles helped to weigh us down, and with these things to hamper us we soon became in a bad mess. To get out was impossible, and to turn back would only make things worse, so we kept on. The mud was getting deeper, and some in front were in difficulties, making those at the rear sink worse through having to halt. The result was that four or five men were up to the waist at the rear. The only way to prevent themselves sinking further was to put their rifles across the top of the trench and rest their chins on them. This was done until another party came and after two hours hard work got them out, more dead than alive.

Well, we got to the firing trench and found that the Germans had been shelling it, and it was not fit for occupation until it had been rebuilt, so we had to come back. The next day we found our time fully occupied in scraping the mud off our clothes to make them a bit lighter, but it was weeks before we got them anything like clean again. This night we were relieved by the Robin Hoods, and when we got back to billets we thanked providence that we had survived the ordeal. It was almost as good as coming back to home. We had four days rest this time and we thoroughly enjoyed every minute of it. After our rest we set out again for the trenches, this time to occupy them. My platoon was told off for a reserve trench, which was more like a small fort. We got there safely, and were comfortably settled down, when we had to shift to the firing trench. This we did on the following night.

The next day we were treated to our baptism of shell fire. It was a funny sensation to hear the shells come over, and although they burst far behind us we all got well down. In the afternoon we had a three hours' series of whiz-bang, coal boxes and shrapnel, but only one came near the trench. This one blew a traverse down under which and some of my chums were sitting. However, beyond smothering us with dirt, no damage was done to any of us.

The next day was fairly quiet, but at night we experienced another kind of projectile. This was the trench mortar. These things cannot be heard coming, and when fired do not make a loud report, and, to make matters worse, they are shot up in the air, so they fall downwards into the trench. They can be seen if watched for by a thin trail of sparks, and the only way to escape them is to watch the direction they are falling and get away from them. If they fall in the trench it wants a few hundred new sandbags. They explode with a terrific report, and if one is unaware of it coming it is a nerve wracking moment. They stopped after a couple of grenades had been sent back in return, and we heard no more of them. The next two days passed without any fresh event, and we were again relieved. This time we had to sleep in a field just behind the line in close reserve for one night. It was very cold, and we had no blankets, but that did not affect us having a good sleep. When we woke in the morning we were issued with a ration of rum, and shortly afterwards marched back to our rest billets.

The next week brought nothing new until we were ordered out one afternoon to take ammunition to the trenches. This was our first good view of the surrounding district by daylight, and very interesting it proved to be. Of course, all is deserted for a few miles behind the lines, and it made things seem very sad to see everything as it was left by the peasants. Fields of corn, vegetables, and tobacco, all running to seed, and here and there a haystack. In one farm that had been razed to the ground there were the bodies of horses, cows and pigs, and in the surrounding fields some sheep and in the garden lay three dogs. These made an abominable smell until they were buried. As we got nearer the trenches there were bodies of French soldiers here and there that up to that time it had been impossible to bury. These were laid to rest shortly afterwards. The houses for the most part still contained their furniture, and the barns were mostly filled with tobacco, hung up to dry. Soon after this we were again in the reserve trenches that I mentioned earlier in this letter, and it was here we experienced some for new sensations. One evening we were told to stand to arms as we were about to blow the German trench up.

At 7pm prompt our artillery opened out in a two hours rapid bombardment, and a few minutes after there was a loud report, followed by an immense column of smoke and flying debris. The earth trembled for miles around. The German big guns were soon in action, but ours had already done their work and that was a score to us the same evening an enemy plane showed itself over our lines (a very unusual occurrence) and one of our airmen was soon up and at him. In a very few minutes the German was a mass of flames, and soon came headlong down, while our fellow sailed serenely back under a terrific fire from the enemy. That was two points to us that day.

The next day we were all sitting about the trench when we felt the earth tremble. We all got to our posts, and found the Germans had attempted to blow our trenches up, but owing to ours being fired first their sap was short, and the consequence was that they did more damage to their own trench than to ours. We were relieved again, and the

Postcards

John & Jenifer Giblin

Embroidered cards such as this one sent by Edwin Jeffery to his mother were
very popular with the troops serving on the Western Front.

John & Jenifer Giblin

A Christmas Card sent by Cotmanhay Church to former members of the choir serving
in the forces, 1917. This one was received by Edwin Jeffery.

Card sent by George Green RAMC October 5th 1916 :
"I am still going on allright and in the best of health and spirit ...
I don't know whether you visit picture houses ...
but the picture which they are showing of the Somme
will give you a good idea what it is like here"

'Forget me not' -
another of the very popular
brightly embroidered cards

next time we went to the trenches we were shifted farther up the line this time we struck a very hot place. my platoon was to garrison a detached trench that was only 25 yards from the enemy, and was only connected to the main trench by a very muddy communication trench. To make matters worse, it was inches deep in mud as usual. We relieved the garrison who were there, and took over our duties. It was a very cheerful aspect to be so close to the enemy and away from our main trench, but we had at least learned to take things as they came, and so we settled ourselves down and prepared to make the best of a bad job.

We got through the night all right, but at dawn we had our first casualty. This was Pte T Wrigley, of Ilkeston, who was looking at a curious part of their trench that he thought was a dug out. He only showed a very small portion of his head, and it was only just half light, but a sniper was watching and poor Tom was hit. It cast a gloom over the rest of the platoon for a long time afterwards. As soon as it got light enough to ensure the Germans would try no attacks we were withdrawn to a support trench in the rear of the line to rest during the day, and this was a Godsend, as it was absolutely impossible for any of us to get any rest during the night. However, we were shelled pretty badly in this trench during the day, but that was by now getting a commonplace incident, so it did not affect our rest.

The next night we took over our trench again. All went well until we had orders to shift at midnight to a new trench. We got to this trench and found it wanting a lot of work before it could possibly be safe. We were too dead beat that night to do anything, so we got down on the bottom, and for the most part mud, and slept. The next day we were all hard at it making the trench something like habitable and by the evening we had it in a better state with a few dug outs. Then we had orders to shift again. That just about did it. Well, the outcome of it all was that night found us back again in our detached post.

An instance of the Germans' "respect" of the Red Cross was visible now that we had a chance to look round. Outside the trench were several of our Highlanders who had fallen when the trench was taken. One party was a grim spectacle. There was a stretcher with a body on it, and the four stretcher bearers lay by the side of it. It appears that the enemy saw this party come out for the wounded and promptly turned a machine gun on to them. It was not safe to go to fetch them in while we were there, although some were fetched in and buried behind the lines with all due reverence. That is only just one instance of German Kultur. Others can be witnessed every day, and at the finish, when all is exposed, Germany will be a shunned nation.

To continue my story, we finished our time in this trench, and were very elated on being released. We were shifted back and again had our rest. The next spell in the trenches was practically without event, until one night we were told that we should be relieved and would have shift further up the line. This time my company were to be in reserve. We started off at night, and at last came to our destination, which proved to be a deserted village situated on a hill just behind the line. It was an eerie place in the darkness. At the end of the place was a tangled heap of smashed barbed wire, which told its own tale of the terrible battle that had taken place before we gained the occupation of the place. All along the main street was scattered debris and bricks from the ruined buildings. We were settled down in houses that had not suffered so badly from the shelling and in the daylight had a scene that beggars description.

The house we had had at one time been a butchers shop, and all the furniture was still there. We rapidly made it into one of the most comfortable billets we had yet had. In all the houses could be seen the remains of household goods which spoke eloquently of the haste with which the inhabitants had left their homes. In the gardens were fruit and vegetables, with which we made some dainty dishes. The only living residents were cats. There were hundreds of them, and a flock of pigeons would now and then circle round the ruins of a farmhouse which probably had once been their home. Then we were able to get a closer view of the place we witnessed the pathos of the whole thing. We could not wander about the place in daylight owing to its prominent position, but at dusk it was possible. There was a blacksmith's shop, with all tools and machinery left just as if they had been in use only a few hours before. This place, save for broken windows, was the only building without a shell hole in it, but the adjoining house was wrecked. The blacksmiths framed certificate lay on the floor undamaged, and underneath a heap of bricks and dust we uncovered a baby's bonnet and here and there were toys. Close by was an old lady's bonnet. One could not but picture his own home in England in the same state if ever the Huns were to get there. In every house could be seen such signs of domestic life and peace mixed up with fragments of implements of war. It was not long before the Germans started their daily practice of shelling the place for an hour, but although some came very close and shook our domicile up, none did any damage.

On our second tour of inspection we discovered a lot of graves, mostly of French soldiers who had fallen in the attack. There was one big cross that covered the graves of 80 Germans. The place was a pathetic picture, and by signs of a railway station and line that ran down the side of the main road it gave one the impression that it had been a pretty summer resort at one time. All around was beautiful scenery, but a distance away the country was scarred and disfigured by trenches. The whole thing was a curious mixture of peace and war, and a picture I am not likely to forget. After a time we left this place, and took over the trenches which proved to be a rather lively set out. We had plenty of shells, and every night the enemy showed great activity, which required us to keep a very close observation on their trenches.

The troops whom we relieved had been having a nice game with the Germans. They had inscribed a banner with the words, "Has anyone seen a German band? With compliments from the Contemptible Little Army", and two or three of them had crawled up to within a short distance of the German parapet and stuck it up. I should have liked to have seen their faces when they saw that little message. It was connected by a wire to our trenches, so if anyone attempted to pull it down we should know, but they did not attempt it while we were in, and it was left flying triumphantly when we left. On relief from this place we were again shifted further up the line and found ourselves in a rest camp that had been used by the Germans, where we rested for a few days before taking over the part of the line we are holding now. Paper will not permit any more being told in this letter, but next time I hope to give you a further account of our adventures.

Ilkeston Advertiser 1st October 1915
Graphic story of a Soldier's Life "Somewhere in France"

Pte H Shaw, of the 5th Sherwoods, whose home is at 139 Station-road, Ilkeston, sends the following graphic account of his experiences to a friend:-

I left off last time where we were in the rest camp. Well, after a few days' enjoyable rest, we were on our way to our new trenches. We were in reserve this time for six days. We had a very long journey to our dug-outs, and for the most part the way was not at all healthy, three or four being wounded, happily not seriously. It was nearing daybreak when we finally arrived at our destination, and most of us simply flung ourselves down and fell asleep without troubling to find dug-outs. These were situated in a large wood just behind the trenches, but they had been occupied for so long that we started the next day to make new ones.

During the day shells were continually passing over our wood, but none dropped near enough to alarm us. The evening found us all ------ [newspaper torn and missing] dead beat after a hard day in new dug-outs. ------ [ditto] next day found us at it again, and ---- [ditto] passed without unusual event. Things remained quiet until tea time of the next day. We were all preparing our tea outside our dug-outs when a heavy high explosive burst just outside the wood. Very little notice was taken of it, as we had been lulled into a sense of security owing to us having no shells near us before. Shortly after another came, dropping slightly closer. Still no notice was taken of it. Shortly after one was heard coming, and something must have deflected its course. It came crashing into the wood, and exploded among a group of our fellows. Five were killed almost instantly, and some 15 were injured. Not a man was unmoved by it, for we had lost some of the best comrades. However, they were laid to rest just with a simple wooden cross on a mound of earth, but heroes' graves for all that. They were well looked after during the rest of the time we were there.

The next three days passed on quietly enough, and we were relieved. We had a weary march to our rest billets, but after a sleep we were all right. The next day we were told we were out for ten days, and that sports and entertainments were being arranged. Those we thoroughly enjoyed. Nothing is more welcome than diversion from the monotony of trench life. The officers all put their hearts in it, and everything went with a swing. One night we had a visit from a pierrot troupe with a piano and the latest songs. We had not heard a piano since landing, and that night amused us more than many a star performance seen in old England. The ten days so passed all too quickly for us, and after the best time we had had out here we packed up for the trenches once more. This time we were in the firing trench, and the six days we were in passed quietly. We were then shifted to a wood just behind the reserve for six days.

These [days] were fairly easy, for we had good dug outs and little work. During this stay we had the satisfaction of seeing an enemy plane brought down. It was set on fire by one of our own pilots. As soon as the enemy observed the plane was doomed he leapt from a great height. We could see him coming down with arms flung out. At last he finished up with a thud close to our wood, where he was found by our fellows. The pilot, however, was forced to keep with the burning plane owing to him being strapped in. The plane volplaned slowly to the earth and landed a mass of flames close by. The airman was burnt beyond recognition.

The German artillery were soon showing their temper, and whizz-bangs were flying all around for some considerable time. When we returned to the fire trench the lull was broken by a big German attack in which action more artillery took part than we had ever heard before. The noise which was on night and day was nerve racking, and we were thankful when we got back to our rest billets after 23 days in the trenches. From then till now things have been just in the ordinary run of the game.

Ilkeston Advertiser 19th November 1915
'The Sherwoods in the Great Advance [The Battle of Loos]

Pte H Shaw, of the 5th Sherwoods, whose home address is 139 Station-road, writes to Mr J W Barton, of Bath-street, Ilkeston, giving a plain and unvarnished account of his adventures in the recent great advance as follows:-

Dear Mr Barton – Just a line to let you know I am still well, and knocking about. I have now another chapter to those I have sent you regarding our adventures. Well, from the finish of my last letter nothing happened out of the ordinary until the morning of the great advance. In this we took no actual part, in the advance, but had our share to do. Our part was to attract the enemy's attention as much as possible in order to blind him as to the real part of the line that the main attack was to be launched, and at the same time to prevent him massing reinforcements on any particular point of the line. To accomplish this we used various devices. We first opened rapid fire, which was accompanied by a heavy bombardment by the artillery. Then bundles of burning straw were thrown over the parapet. The idea in this was to give him the notion that we were using gas. The idea worked with good effect, and the main attack was successful. After that we were shifted to another part of the line, and here our adventures started.

On arrival at our destination we were billeted in a large town just behind the line [*Lens?*], and the sight of the interior brought back many memories of England. Everything was going as usual, trams running and shops carrying on as usual, although the town was liable to be shelled at any minute. We only had one day in this place before we were shifted just outside the town. Here we were settled very comfortable, but not for long, as in a short time we were ordered to pack up at once for a move. In due time we were marched off to meet some motor buses. These were loaded up and away we went just at dusk. After a while we stopped, and were told to get off.

This done we started marching. After a few miles we started getting amongst signs of trouble. First we came upon a heap of dead horses, and the further we went the worse the scenes became. Transports and red cross wagons lay on the side of the road smashed to bits, and here and there were bodies stretched out across our path. We soon entered into a maze of trenches and rightly concluded we were upon the scene of the advance. We were finally placed in an old trench. We lay down in the bottom and slept until daybreak, and the view on awakening beggars description. Everywhere were scenes of the great battle, and it was not long before we were out of the trench searching for souvenirs. This soon brought a few shells over, and for a time we had to keep in the trench. However, we were soon out again, and a good few souvenirs were dispatched home within a few days. Well, after 24 hours in the place we shifted back from the line again.

After a few days' rest, we were told while on parade that our division were to make an attack the next time we went up the line, and this news naturally caused a good deal of excitement amongst us. The next day further details came round, as we learned that our battalion was in reserve in the afternoon we were shown a plan of the trenches to be taken. Two more days and we were on the way to the trenches in fighting order, and at night were settled down in our positions. At 5 am we were called up to take rations to the Brigade who were making the actual charge. We started off, and soon found ourselves in a maze of communication trenches. After taking the wrong turn once or twice, and consequently having to turn back, we found our way to the firing trench and handed our rations over. We were just starting back when our guns started their preliminary bombardment and the return fire of the enemy made it impossible for us to get back, so we just stopped in the fire trench.

At last the time came for the attacking brigade to go over the parapet and this they did like one man. They drove the Germans out of the first line and then we got our share of shells in the old line. We had a lively time dodging them for the next two hours. At last we risked the journey and started back to join the battalion. We met them coming up the communication trench, and as we had to go back to fetch our haversacks and water bottles we got in a small trench to allow them to pass. They were almost past when the enemy found our communication trench with a few gas shells. Of course, we had to double back quickly to get clear of it, so that delayed us a bit more. It was getting on for midnight when we did get our kit, but we got it and started to find our battalion, who were in support in the old firing trench. We found them in the early hours of the morning, and for the rest of the day we were having a hot time with the shells. The next morning we had to go and garrison the captured trench. It was a sight never to be forgotten. Bodies lay in the bottom of the trench (or what was left of it) three thick. It was the most gruesome spectacle I have yet seen.

Our boys and Germans lay together, some blown to pieces and some with no wound visible. Outside it was worse, wounded lay where it was impossible to get them in or to attend to them. The dug-outs were 30ft below the ground, and were practically uninjured. In these we found a stock of clean clothes, etc. in fact it was a small stores. Souvenirs, however, had no attraction for us, and we had our hands full watching and swapping bombs with the enemy, but we never allowed him to get anywhere near our trenches. At night, just as we were being relieved, the enemy attempted a bomb attack, and we were soon pumping rapid fire into them. It would have gone very hard with "Fritz" and "Carl" if they had come right up to the trench, for it was packed with men. After a bit of excitement we were relieved, and marched to our billets half asleep. Two days later we were thanked by the General who praised us very highly.

Well, we were comfortably settled in billets, and on the 28th were all inspected by the King. During our rest I have met another Ilkestonian, in the person of Pte Billy Shaw, of the RAMC, who has been out here for over twelve months. You can guess we spend some pleasant evenings together exchanging adventures and calling back old times together. Well, I shall have to close, as the light is fading, and candles are not very plentiful.'

Letter from an anonymous soldier of the 1st/5th Sherwood Foresters who survived the first day of the Battle of the Somme, as printed in the 'Ilkeston Pioneer', July 14th 1916 :

"IN A SHELL-HOLE FOURTEEN HOURS.

One of the Ilkeston Terriers has sent an interesting letter to his parents, from No. 4 Convalescent Depot, Havre, in the course of which he says :

"You will have heard of the big battle of July 1st. Well, we took an active part in it, and suffered severe losses. I am a lucky lad, for I came through with two slight shrapnel wounds, one in the back and the other in the right thigh. I can walk about all right, so you can tell I am not bad. It is not quite bad enough to get me to England. We went over at 7.30am on Saturday morning, and I was wounded while in the German first line, and I tried to get back to our own lines. But the machine gun and shell fire was so bad that I had to stay in a shell-hole for cover.

I had to stay there until 10 o'clock at night, when I made a dash under cover of dark, and reached our own lines. I found the battalion – or what was left of them – had been relieved. I found them out, before I reported to have my wounds dressed, for I was anxious to know who had come through. It was a terrible shock when I found only six of my platoon were all right. Of course, a lot had gone through the advanced dressing station, wounded; but we had a lot killed. There will be some sad homes in Ilkeston and Derby.

Sergt [Henry] Shaw was killed, and I am afraid Bert Spiby as well. He was missing, but no-one had seen him so far as I could find out. I was the only one of our company to turn up. CSM Benson was wounded. I am afraid Joe Bacon was killed. Corpl E. Fletcher is another Ilkeston lad who was wounded. I heard Jimmy Atkins had gone under, but can't say for sure. Among others missing in the same platoon as myself were Alf. Edwards, Freddy German and E. White. I know White comes from Ilkeston, but don't know where he lives. Well, I was sent off to hospital where I had my wounds dressed and was inoculated; and after spending Sunday night in Hospital I was put on the hospital train and sent down to this convalescent camp, where I am now. It was very nice on the hospital train. You lay there in bed, looking out of the window, and there were English Nurses to look after us, and they brought us papers to read and brought us our meals.

The train seemed like a palace, and we were the honoured guests. On the station where we were waiting for the train a lady came to us and gave us bread and butter and tea and some fags. She seemed like an angel moving about among the wounded. There were hundreds of poor chaps who were very badly wounded. I learned afterwards that she was Miss Boot, daughter of Jesse Boot the chemist. We were on the train from 9 o'clock on Monday night until 6 o'clock on Tuesday night.

While I lay in the shell-hole on Saturday, I was only 80 yards from the Germans and I dare not even turn over, or I should have been spotted, and they would have fired at me. They turn machine-guns on our poor wounded chaps who lay out between the lines. Another Ilkeston Sergt (Sergt. Henson) is missing."

Ilkeston Pioneer, 14th July 1916

'One of the victims of the 'Great Push' was Serjeant Henry Shaw of the Sherwoods (son of Mr Arthur Shaw, 139 Station-road Ilkeston) of whose death there is unfortunately not a shadow of a doubt. That he had fallen has been mentioned in the letters of several of his comrades who have written home and one of them has informed Shaw's parents that he performed the last sad office for him by seeing to his interment.

Shaw was only 21 and was a smart and fearless soldier. He was promoted Serjeant on the field and whilst in France wrote several interesting letters to the local papers. Since going out he had only one short period of leave from the 17th to 19th December last. When war broke out he was working as a miner at West Hallam Colliery. He was of a cheerful disposition, and made many friends.

His parents have been in receipt of a number of letters of sympathy. Amongst them is one from Mrs Katherine J. Hutchinson of 2 Spenser-road Harpenden with whom the young soldier was billeted during the lengthy period his regiment remained at that place. It is of a very touching character, and the sentiments it expresses do credit to the lady who wrote it. We give the following extracts from it :

"I cannot tell you how grieved we are to hear that your dear son, Henry, has been killed in this awful war. I feel it as if he were my own, and for your great sorrow, I have most heartfelt sympathy. He was such a dear lad and I know will have died most bravely and gloriously for his country. All honour to him! You must in the midst of all your sorrow feel immensely proud of him.

It is a sad time. Day by day we hear of friends gone. Harpenden has several to mourn this week. The mothers are wonderfully brave, as the sons would wish them to be. I know, and bear up for the sake of the rest of your family. We got to know him so well, all the weeks he was with us, and I always hoped he would live to return home safely, and that we might see him again.

The bronze Memorial Plaque, often known as the 'Dead Man's Penny', was given to the families of British servicepeople who died during the war.

A much rarer female version was produced with an 'S' added to make 'SHE' rather then 'HE'. In total 1,355,000 plaques were issued, which used a total of 450 tonnes of bronze.

The design of the plaque, which is about five inches (120 mm) in diameter, was chosen through a public competition. Over 800 designs were submitted and the winner was sculptor and medallist Edward Carter Preston with his design called 'Pyramus', which won him £250.

Memorial Plaques continued to be issued into the 1930s to commemorate those who died as a consequence of the war.

They were usually issued together with the memorial scroll from King George V, as shown earlier in this book.

This Plaque commemorates Richard Elliott, our first known local casualty.

Only a week ago I sent him a parcel and wrote to congratulate him on being a sergeant. Probably he never received it, as when the push began I expect it was difficult to get the letters and parcels delivered.

Have you any news of his friend Zeke Smith? They were so much together that Zeke would be dreadfully cut up, I'm sure".'

Ilkeston Pioneer, 14th July 1916

"Private Ezekiel Smith, who figures among the wounded is a son of Mr Ed. Smith the well known old Manners Colliery cricketer of 26 Station-road Ilkeston and his injuries are confined to his left arm, in which he has been shot.

He was over home on leave five weeks ago and is 22 years of age being employed in the Manners Colliery when war commenced. A postcard was received from him on Thursday of last week stating that he had been wounded; and the fact has also been mentioned in letters from several of his comrades."

Sam Kidger's letters

Samuel Kidger fought in Egypt, Palestine, Belgium and France and was torpedoed on the SS *Transylvania* off Italy. Many of his letters home to his brother and sister (but not to his new wife, Harriett) have survived and we print some extracts here, with thanks to his great-nephew David Kirk for transcribing them :

APRIL 25th 1917 WITH THE BRITISH EXPEDITIONARY FORCE

Dear Bro and Sister, Just a few lines to let you know that I am alright and in the best of health. We have had a train ride of 48 hours without a change and have gone into another rest camp before we embark again. I might tell you the scenery of France is lovely, we went through vineyards by the acre the hills and the rivers are splendid. The weather over here is grand, just like summer in England. We sit outside our tents in our shirtsleeves looking at the blue sea. Our camp is on the hillside and there are black as well as white troops here. […] We are living an easy life in these rest camps, all we have to do is bask in the sun. I hope Harriett is alright, you must try and keep her cheerful, […] I should like to get an English paper now and again for to buy one here costs 2d for one sheet, how would you like to pay that? You can get Tobacco and Cigarettes very cheap in our camp. Beer is very dear so I am TT. I shall have lots to tell you when I get home again for you see we are not allowed to write what we should like to but I might say that we are having the time of our lives and we all think we are very lucky to be on this draft. We have a good Officer, a happy go lucky sort and I think all the men admire him. So I think that it is all this time, hoping to hear from you sometime. Your Loving Bro Sam

UNDATED 42 551 2/7 GARR BATTALION NORTHUMBERLAND FUSILIERS,
ARMY REST CAMP NO 8 c/o ARMY PG NO 7 BEF FRANCE

Dear Bro and Sister,

Just a few lines to let you know that I am alive and well which is something to be thankful for after what I have gone through. We were having a splendid voyage when all at once we were struck by two tin fish and then the sight was awful but I managed to pull through alright but I will tell you all when I come back home again. […] You cannot write what you would like to BUT if you see anything in the papers that happened on May 4th you will know that I was on it and then you will know what I mean. Let them all know that you have heard from me and tell Harriett I will write to her next, you see we cannot get writing paper or else I would write oftener for we have nothing to do but lie in the shade. Remember me to all I remain Your Loving Bro Sam. Still keeping my pecker up.

MAY 29th 1917 IN FRANCE   [The sinking of the SS *Transylvania*]

Dear Bro and Sister,

[...] No doubt you will have seen by now what ship I was on, it was a very large one. When the first torpedo hit her I was down below and it put all the lights out and when I got on the deck some of the boats was leaving the ship with the Nurses on board. A JTBD [Japanese Torpedo Boat destroyer] had just drew alongside and was taking men off when I saw a second torpedo coming through the water and it was worse than the first and then the order was "Every Man Overboard". It was awful, we could not launch no more boats, the rafts we threw overboard to the men in the water. I was on the point of jumping in also. I had took my boots and puttees off when I saw a second JTBD coming alongside and I jumped on to her as she was passing us. I might say that there was hundreds saved like that, all honour to the Japs who are brave men. I also saw men fall between both ships and were crushed to death. I shall never forget it. I got off 10 minutes before she sank. I am pleased to say that we landed in sunny Italy and the people gave us a great welcome. They gave us wine, Ciggs, Cigars and such beautiful flowers and I had to walk through the town bare footed and now we are again in France the place we started from. […] Tell Harriett I am writing to her tomorrow as we are only allowed to write once a day. Hoping all of you are in the best of health, also those at home. I remain Your Loving Bro Sam

JUNE 16th 1917 CAIRO

Dear Bro and Sister,

Just a few lines to let you know that I am alive and well and I hope you are also. We are in Barracks on the banks of the Nile and we are getting good food but the climate is very hot in the daytime but very nice at night. We do all our work early in the morning getting up at 0530 and have finished by 1000 for the day. We wear helmets and our clothes are like overalls, the trousers are what they call shorts, like football knickers. After we left Marseilles we were 9 days on the water and no doubt it would be fine in peacetime but it is not very pleasant now with these tin fish knocking about. We had one attack just as we were having our tea but our Destroyers kept them off this time. We had 2 days in Messina which they are rebuilding. I have not been into the City yet, only when we marched through. It seems strange to see the men dress like women and some of the women have their faces covered over and they wear something that covers their nose. We landed at Alexandria and then we took train for Cairo. […] We can see the Pyramids from our Barracks and I shall go and have a look around them when I have the chance. We can get a pint of beer for 5d, what is the price at home now? Eggs are very cheap, also fruit. I think that is about all this time, hoping you are all in the best of health. Give my love to all at home. I remain Your Loving Bro Sam

JUNE 24th 1917 ANZAC HOSTEL

Dear Bro and Sister,

Just a few lines to let you know that I am still alright. I went to the Pyramids yesterday, Sat and I enjoyed myself very much. It is about 7 miles from here and we go on the car to them. It is wonderful how ever they got the great slabs of stone there. I have been through the Museum which is a very fine building and some lovely works of art inside and there are also mummies which you can see for yourself. Hundreds of years old the Kings of this country with the flesh on their bones to the present day. It is a wonderful city is Cairo, you see some of the men with their wives I might tell you that they have more than one and they drive them about with a donkey and cart, then there are men driving their camels through the streets with loads on their backs. I like this place alright although very hot in the day time but cooler than England in the summer at night. In the room that I am in they are mostly Scotsmen and it is very amusing to hear them talk when we are hunting for the bugs and I am sorry to say they are very plentiful and they keep you company at night. [...] You must let me have all the news when you write back, give my love to all at home. Wishing you all the best of luck, also Good Health. I remain Your Loving Bro Sam

June 27th 1917 KASR EL NILE CAIRO

Dear Bro and Sister,

[...] I wish the war was over and I was back home again but I am sorry to say that it seems a long way from being finished yet but we shall have to hope for the best. You asked me if I got into the water which I am pleased to say that I did not although I had gone down a rope to do so but I saw there was a danger of being killed by the rafts which they were throwing overboard and was falling on the men in the water. So I got back on board again and then I had the good luck to jump on a Jap Destroyer which came alongside. We tried to launch some of the boats that was left but could not do so as we did not understand them, you see all the crew had gone with the other boats and we had to do the best for ourselves, it was every man for himself. [...] Give my love to all, trusting you will all have good luck. I remain your loving Brother Sam

AUGUST 4th 1917 CAIRO

Dear Bro and Sister,

Just a few lines in answer to your letters and newspapers which I received today. I have been away from Cairo for one week up the line guarding a Railway Swing Bridge, so I got them when I got back. I thank you very much for the five shillings that you sent me and I shall send Doris a Bead Necklace there are some lovely things over here but you see it is risky sending them over. [...] What price is the eggs now, they are very cheap over here, you can get 4 for 1 piastre the value in English 2 1/2d. I have had for breakfast every morning while on this guard eggs, tomatoes and bacon fried, we had brought the eggs and tomatoes we had given us and we cooked our own. It was rather amusing to watch the native men and women come to the river to wash, after the men have washed they say their prayers and they always face the East and they do it three times a day. The women come to wash themselves their clothes which they put on again while they are wet and also to carry water back with them which they carry in large stone jars on their heads, it is surprising how they do it. The best sport we have is with the children who come and talk to us, they try to learn English and we try to learn their language, we get along very well. We point to things and say English so and so and then they point to the same thing and say Arabic so and so and that is how we do it. [...] Give my love to all. Shall be pleased when I am home again. I remain your loving Bro Sam

AUGUST 13th 1917 CAIRO

Dear Bro and Sister,

[...] I might say that the prettiest places I saw was when we were running down the Italian Coast to Messina, it was lovely, I only hope I shall get back some day to tell you all about it. You ask me about the bugs and wonder if Keatings would shift them but I am sorry to say that I don't, you see there are millions of them and to beat them we lie on the verandah outside [...]. Was very pleased to hear of you having a good crop in the garden and I should have liked very much to have been at home to have had my dinner of new peas and potatoes, no doubt you would have enjoyed them very much. I only hope Old Moores speaks the truth this time for to tell you the truth I am tired of living away from home and shall be only too pleased to get back home again. I went out on pass yesterday, Sunday to have a free tea which they give every Sunday to soldiers at the Gardens and at a large block of buildings called the Anzac Hotel which is a place where they billet troops from down the line, it is like a YMCA. Well I went to this place along with three other young men and we had a splendid tea as much as we could eat, all kinds of pastry and sandwiches. My word we did shift some. Plenty of tea to drink. I had to let my belt out to be able to sing for we had a short service after tea and we sang some of the old Hymns that we used to sing at home and I quite enjoyed it, shall go again if possible. Then we went a walk around the city, places what we should call the Slums, you see some funny sights and strange ways the natives have, we went into a place were they was weaving cloth all being done with hands and feet, it is wonderful how they do it and then we saw a large wedding, men on

Both : Grant Shaw

Left : Mapperley's War Memorial takes the form of a lytch gate to the churchyard

Right : We will remember them ... The annual ceremony of remembrance at the Park Cemetery CWGC memorial in Ilkeston.

camels beating drums, two men on the front carrying large looking glasses on long poles, also a bagpipe band and a brass one too then came more camels with a kind of a house on two of them carrying the bride inside, after that came carriages with black horses bringing his other wives and children of which there was plenty. [...]
I remain your loving Bro Sam

AUGUST 25th 1917 THE YMCA WITH THE EGYPTIAN EXPEDITIONARY FORCES

Dear Bro and Sister,

[...] we can fish in the Nile if we like but I care nothing about it for it looks so muddy. It is a very large river and is very deep and runs very fast. There are lots of House Boats up near to us. You say that they are going to fetch a lot of the young men out of the Pits, well I think that they cannot grumble at that for there are thousands of young single men left there and you find lots of men, forty and upwards in the Army, a long way from being just. [...] I hope and trust that this war will soon be over and I can get home again for there is no place like Old England. [...] Give my love to all, wishing you all the best of luck. I Remain your Loving Bro Sam

SEPTEMBER 2nd 1917 CAIRO

Dear Bro and Sister,

Just a few lines to let you know that I am still going on alright but sorry to say that I will not be here much longer, I might go away any day now. [...] How I wish the war was over and I was coming back again for I am tired of being away from home. This climate over here is hot, I have not seen any rain since I came here, so you will have a bit of idea what it is like. At Night time it is very cold and there is a heavy dew and with lying outside we have our water proof sheet on the top of us and that is wet through when we get up in the morning. So I expect that if I ever get back to England it will mean a few Doctor's bills. [...] I have some lovely things over here which are made by Turkish Prisoners and if I have the luck to come back home from here I shall try and bring a few things back with me. I have enjoyed myself fairly well these last few weeks with having a few games at Cricket for at every match you get a free tea, what they call over here a Buckshee and I am going this afternoon to one at the Anzac Hostel, far nicer than having Bread and Jam which is our usual fare, we never see any butter in the Barracks. Well I think that is all this time, hoping all are well, give my love to all, keep Harriett as cheerful as you can.
I remain Your Loving Bro Sam

SEPTEMBER 10th 1917 EGYPT   (Sam has been transferred to the Scottish Rifles)

Dear Bro and Sister,

[...]At the present time I am in a Camp on the banks of the Suez Canal which is a wonderful piece of work, it runs right through the Desert. I am sorry to tell you that I am on the way to the firing line and I only hope that I shall have the good luck to go through all right. I wonder when this will finish for I think that every one is about fed up with it, how pleased we all shall be to get back home again. 52 0221/8 SCOTTISH RIFLES. This all the change in my address. We do not wear kilts but we have Scotch Bonnets and I only hope that I shall the pleasure of coming home in it. [...] There are no houses where I am, only desert and all you can see is only sand. If I only have the luck to get back home again I shall have lots to tell you about Egypt. I am to be inoculated again this afternoon, a bit more pain but it will not last for ever. It is a good job that Jim is out of it for I am sure he would not be able to stand it for it is a hard life. I think that is all this time, give my love to all at home. I remain Your Loving Bro Sam

SEPTEMBER 19th 1917 EEJ EGYPT

Dear Bro and Sister, I am sending you a few lines to let you know that I am alright up to now. I am still in this camp on the banks of the Suez Canal but expect being sent up any day now for I have been inoculated twice this week. I hope and trust that I shall have the good luck to come through alright and be able to meet you all again, won't there be some rejoicing then for some and broken hearts for others. It is about time the war was over for I think everybody is about fed up with it. I am sorry to say that I have had no letters for 3 weeks from anyone but I expect it is through leaving Cairo but I shall get them all at the same time later on. So keep on writing to me but do not send any money for it be no use to me up the line. I hope you are keeping Harriett as cheerful as you can for she is bound to be upset when she knows that I am going into danger. But I am trusting to one above to pull me through and I think he will do so. [...]

I remain your loving Bro Sam

SEPTEMBER 30th 1917 IN THE DESERT

Dear Bro and Sister,

In answer to your letter which I received today, also three lots of papers and a lot of other letters for you so I did not get any for about six weeks. I was very pleased to hear that you was all in good health and that Jim was playing with Chilwell and I hope he made a good score. I have had several games while I was in Cairo but find it a lot different to playing at home, the wickets are much faster for you see they play on coco matting. I was pleased that you had got the photo alright and that you thought it was a good one of me. So you think I look a little thinner than I used to be, well I feel no worse for it. [...] I am living in a Dug Out just behind the firing line where we can see the shells bursting so you will see by that there is a bit of fighting in Palestine. I only hope I have the good luck to come through alright and then I shall have a lot to tell you what I have seen when I get back again. I shall not be sorry when the war is over for over here all we can see is sand, no houses or anything. It gets on your nerves what with the heat and the sand, I am about fed up with it. I am sorry to hear that stout is so dear, no doubt you feel a bit lost without it. I myself have drunk more water since I have been in the Army than all the rest of my life. [...] Give my love to all, tell them I hope to see them all again someday. Thanking you for all your kindness, keep Harriett cheerful. I remain Your Loving Brother Sam

OCTOBER 9th 1917 IN THE FRONT LINE TRENCHES IN PALESTINE

Dear Bro and Sister,

[…] Yes I had some good times while I was in Cairo and I was very sorry to have to leave it for where I am now we have to live in the ground and you know it is not like being in Barracks. We are always under fire as we are waiting "Johnny's Pleasure" for I think he will get a surprise some day. […] What a blessing it will be when it is all over, how pleased everyone will be. [...] I was very pleased to hear that Doris liked the beads that I sent and if I have the luck to see the finish of the war which I am hoping to do I shall try and get you all something to bring back. You all seem to think that I have got thinner, well to tell you the truth I do not feel a bit worse for it. I had a bathe in the Sea last Sunday for we had marched to another part of the line and I might tell you it is hard work carrying your pack across the Desert. It is far healthier here for we get the sea breeze and you feel as if you could eat anything. We get a loaf of bread a man, Bully Beef, Jam and Stew and we are hundreds of miles from any town, it has all to come across the Desert, it is wonderful what the British Army can do, it makes you to feel proud to be an Englishman. Well I think that is all this time, I am glad that you are keeping Harriett cheerful. Wishing you all the Best of Health and Luck. Give my love to all I remain Your Loving Bro Sam

OCTOBER 23rd 1917 IN PALESTINE

Dear Bro and Sister,

[...] Well I am pleased to say that I am in the best of health for we are in a very healthy place just being camped at the Seaside, but by the letter that I have sent home you will see all about it [...]. I hardly know what to write about for it is all one thing over here which is no light task marching over the desert. The heat in the daytime is unbearable but at night it is bitter cold, in fact you cannot keep warm. The best thing that I enjoy is a bath in the sea, the water is quite warm and it does you a world of good. I was on water escort duty the other day, we have camels to carry it across the desert, we had 43 camels to look after and they are only a few for there are hundreds of them and they give them a wash in the sea, it is quite amusing to watch them. In this camp we are still under shell fire, we had a lot dropping around us this morning but we are getting used to it by now. I only hope I shall have the good luck to come through it alright and get back home safe again. Give my love to all. Look after Harriett. Your loving Bro Sam

SATURDAY OCTOBER 27th 1917 IN PALESTINE

Dear Bro and Sister,

I answer to your two letters of 26th Sept and Oct 6th, I got the last one the first but I am sorry to say that I have not received that Testament yet but I will let you know when I do. [...] Believe me it seems so nice to get a letter from home and to hear the news, for you see we are miles from nowhere [...]. It is very hard work marching across the Desert, you feel sometimes as if you could lay down and die and every day is alike. But it is all done for a purpose and that is to be able to chase the Turks when we have driven them out of their position. I was very sorry to hear about the explosion at Chilwell it was a blessing that it happened at night when there was not so many at work. I was very pleased to hear of Willie looking so well and I hope he will never have to leave England, for if ever I get back again I shall take good care that I don't. Have they taken any men out of the Pits yet for I think they are lucky men to be at home while we are going through it. So you have been having Air Raids, we have them every day, we take no notice of them now although the guns are firing at them all the time but I will tell you all about it when I get home again. I think that is all this time, thanking you for your kindness. I trust you are all in the best of health, also those at home. Give my love to all. I remain your loving Bro Sam

MONDAY 5th NOVEMBER 1917 IN PALESTINE

Dear Bro and Sister,

In answer to your letter which I received last Thursday night just before we went into action. I was very pleased to hear from you, I think the cards were very nice, you might thank Mrs Baker for them for me. I put them in my pocket along with the Testament and I think one above must have watched over me. It was a trying time, you would think it almost impossible to live in charging the Trenches. The shot and shell was flying all directions and after we got into the Turkish Lines we were under fire all the time both day and night. We can see that town what we are going to take quite plain now, all of this country seems full of cactus plants and they grow 7 or 8 feet high. Then there are a lot of fruit trees and then trenches we have taken run all amongst them and we are being sniped at all day long. We came out of the Trenches this morning for the first time since taking them and it has been very hard work, for you see you have to build and fight both night and day and we been short of water for a little while, but things are improving now. [...]You must excuse me not writing more but I am so very tired, had very little sleep for three nights but I will write more next time, so give my love to all, thanking you again for the papers that you are sending me. I smoked those Cigs, the first for a long while. I Remain Your Loving Brother Sam

PS The night we went into action we had a drink of Rum. We had the Navy and the Tanks helping us. We took what is known as EL ARRISH REDOUBT.

DECEMBER 11th 1917 IN PALESTINE

Dear Bro and Sister,

[...] I have seen a bit more of the world since I wrote to you last. We have covered a good many miles since we got the Turks on the run. We have left the Desert behind now and we are among the orange trees, the Jaffa ones and I have eaten a good many. We are having very wet weather now and we have no shelter at all. Very often you cannot lay down at night for the ground is like a pond and you have to do the best you can. You dry your clothes on your back. I hope I do not get Jim's complaint for my legs are awful. Well it will soon be Xmas and a poor one for me but I wish you all a Merry one and a Happy New Year. Well I think that is all, I could write a lot more but I have not the time. Give my love to all. I Remain Your Loving Bro Sam.

141

Grant Shaw

The Loos Cemetery and Memorial just outside Lens in the coalfields near the Belgian Border. Did the spoil heaps and the headstocks which used to dot the landscape in this barren industrial plain remind those who had been miners in civilian life of their homes in the Erewash Valley? The memorial commemorates 20,620 men who died in this area during the war and who are still 'missing'; their names are carved on the walls of the enclosure.

FEBRUARY 9th 1918 IN PALESTINE

Dear Bro and Sister,

[…] I am pleased to say that I received your Xmas boxes, also card and the parcel of Ciggs which Jim sent […] I see by the papers you are doing your share of suffering in England, what a blessing it will be when this war is over. I am pleased to say that we cannot grumble out here for we get rations every day although some days are a bit worse than others. [...] Is Jim still at work at Chilwell for it is the shells which is winning the war. [...] Give my love to all, wishing you all the best of health, I remain your loving Brother Sam.

Tell them that I am writing to them all. How would an orange go down?

FEBRUARY 15th IN PALESTINE

Dear Bro and Sister,

[...] I am so sorry that you have had no letters from me for a long while I know that I have not written many, but you must forgive me for it has been no fault of mine. After we had taken Gaza of which I sent you my experience of going over the top but it looks as if you did not receive it, we had to go after the Turks, then we had a lot of wet weather. I was very often wet through and we had no dry clothes to put on, then to make matters worse I got all my writing paper and envelopes spoilt so I could not write without begging paper and then there was a lot more like me. I am pleased to say that I received all the parcels that you sent me, also the ciggs that Jim sent for which I thank you, but the best thing that you can do is every time you write, put a bit of writing paper and an envelope inside then I shall be able to answer it [...].

I feel so sorry to hear of you all having to stand hours in the street waiting for food and then very often not being able to buy any, what a blessing it will be when the war is over. We are doing very well for food, we get some every day and just lately we have been having Rabbits. Well I am pleased to say that I am in good health and still amongst the oranges of which there are plenty [...]. I only hope I shall have the luck to come home again and I will try and re pay you all for your kindness which I will never forget. So remember me to Mrs Baker and thank her for the Testament for I often look at it and think about you all at Ilkeston. Give my love to all, I remain your loving Bro Sam

MARCH 5th 1918 IN PALESTINE

Dear Bro and Sister,

[...] Well I am pleased to say that I am alright up to now, for I am still in the same place which I have wrote and told you about. We are getting good food, Fresh meat and Rabbits, very often butter and bread most days, so we cannot grumble, for I often think of the poor people at home, how they must be suffering having to stand all those hours in the streets waiting for food, and then very often not getting any. What a blessing it will be when this war is over, but we must stick it till we have smashed the Huns. [...]

We are having lovely weather out here, just like our summer. The trees are full of blossom and the fields are covered with flowers. The Natives are working in the fields, ploughing the ground and sowing the corn. For drawing the plough they use Oxen and Donkeys just the same as they did hundreds of years ago. The women out here work very hard, in fact they do it about all for a lot of the men sit on the river bank fishing all day, I must admit it is very nice fish for I have had some. [...]

I remain your loving Brother Sam (finish orange)

APRIL 9th 1918 ON BOARD SHIP SS CANBERRA ALEXANDRIA

Dear Bro and Sister, Just a few lines in answer to your letter of March 14th which I received on board this ship. [...] Very sorry to hear of Willie being in the trenches again for I know how hard it is but I do hope that he will have good luck and come through alright. [...] Now as regards myself at the time of writing this letter I am aboard the ship and we are lying in Alexandria and I think we are bound for the same place where Willie is. There is a whole Division going, so I expect that we shall have some more hard times. I hope and trust that we shall get across safely this time, for this morning there was a convoy of Merchant Ships went out and one got sunk about 15 miles out and the rest have all come back again. When we got orders that we were leaving Palestine we were lying in a little village the name of which was Farona[?] then we marched to a place called Lud where we got on the train and we rode in wagons down to Kantara. Got out there and had a few hours rest and then we marched across the Suez Canal and got on the train again. Wagons again bound for Alexandria. We are travelling two nights and one day and then we got right on the Ship CANBERRA. So good bye to Egypt and Palestine. We are all wondering if we shall get a leave before we go on this new front for a lot of the men in the 52 Division have been out for three years, they were at the Dardanelles so I think it is about time they had one. Well I think that is about all this time, hoping this letter will find you all in the best of health [...] Your Loving Bro Sam

APRIL 22nd 1918 IN FRANCE

Dear Bro and Sister,

[…] You will see by this that I am in a fresh country and we find it very cold after being used to warm weather. [...] We had a rough voyage in coming over a good many being sea sick, but am pleased to say we got across safely this time. We landed at the same place where I was at before [Marseilles] then we were riding three days and nights in the train in trucks. […] I see that they are extending the age limit, there will be a good many to come now who never thought they would ever be called upon. [...] I have not heard from home for a long while so I expect that there letters have got lost on the way. but am expecting to hear from them every day now. Yes it was perhaps for the best that Willie got in hospital for no doubt he would have been in this great battle which is on now. Shall write to him today, I hope he is going on alright. No doubt you will all be surprised to know that I am in France. I only hope that I shall have good luck to come through alright and get back home safe again. So wishing you all the best of health and luck. Your Loving Bro Sam

MAY 4th 1918 IN FRANCE

Dear Bro and Sister,

[...] What a blessing it will be when this cruel war is finished for it is causing many a breaking heart, also taking many valuable lives, how is poor Mrs Rice taking the loss of her husband, then there is S Smith, I never thought that they would come to such a poor end, but one never knows what is going to happen. [...] The weather is same thing like it is in England, very little sunshine and plenty of rain and we find it very cool, but I expect it as we have come from a warm climate. [...] I remain your loving Bro Sam

MAY 11th 1918 IN FRANCE

Dear Bro and Sister,

[…] I was very sorry to hear that Redvers had gone [into the army], no doubt you feel it very much but I hope and trust that he will have the best of health and luck and that the war will be over before he has to cross the Channel. [...] You ask me if I have ever met anyone who I know since coming to France, I am sorry to say that I have not, but I have seen a lot of the hellish work the Huns have done, where I am now they have smashed the churches and houses to bits, and I have seen places which before the war was pretty French villages but all that you can see now is a heap of rubbish, then they say pity the Germans. You say that Father and Mother are busy setting the Garden and how nice it would be if I got a leave to come and see it, I might say that is what we are all looking for, for there are a lot of the men who have been away from home almost three years, but there seems no hope of having one yet. [...] So they are being fetched out of the pits now and about time too, they have been very lucky to escape it as long as they have done, no doubt they are pulling long faces now. I hope this letter will find you all in good health as I am pleased to say that I am quite well and getting good food. [...] Well I think that is all the news this time, give my love to all, hoping that the war will soon be finished and that we are all safe back home again. I remain your Loving Bro Sam.

MAY 19th 1918 IN FRANCE

Dear Bro and Sister,

[…] I was very pleased to hear from you and to know that you had been to see Willie from whom I have received a letter telling me that he has not been so well, but it is perhaps all for the best for the longer he stays in England the more trouble he will miss. I have had a PC from Redvers giving me his address to which I have replied, he seems to think that he won't be long before he is in France which I sincerely hope he is mistaken for it is a hard life out here. I am writing this letter on the stairs leading down into a large room underground which was made by the Huns out of which they were driven by the Canadians a long while ago. I cannot describe the country here for it is all smashed up. All the houses are lying in ruins, even the trees are blown to bits. The ground is all full of shell holes and the guns are going night and day and we get very little rest, although we are safe from shellfire down in the dugout. But there is always the danger of Gas and we always have our gas helmets around our necks ready to put on for you never know when he is going to send it over. I am very sorry to hear of Redvers arm being so painful but I have gone through it myself so I know what it is. How I wish this war would finish, to bring all this suffering to end. [...] How is Frank going on, he seems to have nothing but bad luck and I feel very sorry for him. Some times I wish that I was like him so that I could be at home for I am fed up with this life. Some times I think the war will never finish for I am longing to get home again, if only to do a bit of gardening. […] We can only hope for the best, Sunny Days will come again. [...] I remain Your Loving Bro Sam

JUNE 4th 1918 IN FRANCE

Dear Bro and Sister,

[...] I am pleased to say that I have come out of the Trenches for a rest, we are lying just behind the firing line and last night I went to the Pictures and I enjoyed them very much for your mind is taken off the war while you are there. We are having very nice weather out here now but we find it very cold at night but it is not so bad for we are living in huts and they are far nicer than being down in deep dugouts. Very pleased to hear that you have a better chance of getting food now for I am sure that you can do with it after being such a long while with so small amount and I hope things will go on improving. Well I am pleased to say that I am in good health and I trust that you are all well at Ilkeston. So give my love to all at home [...]. I remain, Your Loving Bro Sam

Dear Bro and Sister,

[...] Well I am pleased to say that I am out of the line for a short rest, our Batt was relieved a few days ago. I never had so hard a time in all my life as we had while we were in the Trenches, we had very little rest, we had to stand to every night and morning in case the Huns should make an attack, then after we had done that we had to start to work and always under shell fire and very often gas, and that meant putting on your helmet, then he would send some shells over which would burst into flames, so you see it is not a very easy life out here. I only wish that we could see the end of it in sight but I am sorry to say that there seems no hopes of that yet. [...]Well I am pleased to say that I am alright up to now and in good health, all that I am longing for is for this cruel war to finish and I am safe back home again, for you never know the value of a good home till you are taken away from it. [...]
So wishing you all the best of health and luck. Your Loving Bro Sam

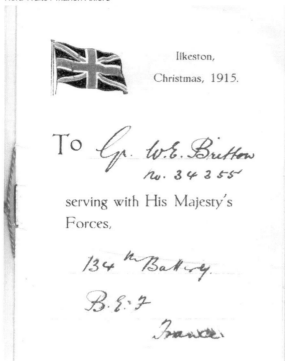

Ilkeston,
Christmas, 1915.

To Gr. W.E. Britton
No. 34355

serving with His Majesty's Forces,

134th Battery

B.E.F

France.

To each and all of you whether on sea or on land, your old town from a full heart sends the old glad greeting~"A Merry Christmas."
Our thoughts are always and gratefully with you, for we are proud of you – proud that with a clear consciousness of duty you have taken up arms for the defence of all you hold dear and have quitted you like men.
You will deserve, and you will receive the respect and reverence of all who honour valour, love virtue and speak truth.
We had wished that you might have spent Christmas at home with us but as that may not be, we send you, for remembrance. these sights of the old town, and the message "Be of good Hope."
All of us – your fellow townsfolk from the old in years to the little children have joined to provide the cheer we ask you to accept.
A Merry Christmas! May a speedy and glorious victory crown your arms and may you soon come back safe to home and friends again.

CHRISTMAS 1916.

ILKESTON

TO HER BRAVE SOLDIER AND SAILOR SONS WHO ARE NOW SERVING THEIR KING AND COUNTRY IN DEFENCE OF JUSTICE FREEDOM AND RIGHTEOUSNESS.

Borough of Ilkeston.

Christmas, 1917.

Ilkeston Corporation sent a Christmas Card to local people serving abroad.

JUNE 16th 1918 IN FRANCE

Dear Bro and Sister,

[...]. You say that you wish that I was out of it, but you cannot wish any more than I do, for how men stand this life in the winter I really do not know for now, and it is supposed to be warm weather. As you are standing on guard in the Trench at night watching No Mans Land you cannot keep warm, and you lie down the same as you stand up only you have a waterproof sheet to sleep on, you go to sleep cold and you wake up cold. You can get your best sleep in the daytime when the sun is shining for you are nice and warm then and we get down on the fire step when not on duty and go to sleep, never troubling about shells which are continually going over us and bursts like thunder all night and day, and it is surprising how used you get to it.

So sorry to hear of Redvers being so ill, but you get no pity in the Army, they seem to think that man is only a machine, but they will get a rude awakening when the war is over, the men are longing for it to finish so that they can get back home again and to get a little pleasure. We cannot complain about our food although some days it takes us all our time to make it last the day out. That is caused by transport mishaps which cannot be avoided. Then we get a drop of Rum now and again, I had mine this morning in my tea and it went down fine. I hope and trust that Redvers will soon be better, but the longer he is in hospital the better it will be for him, and it is the same as you say, he is like Jim, he is not very strong and it would have been better if he could have stayed at his work, but I am sorry to say there are a lot like him in the Army now and theirs is a life of misery.[...] This week we had a surprise gift of Ciggs, they were sent by the people of America to the Allied Armies, so you see that they mean business. I am in the Trenches again, a little further to the [censored] this time but still at the same place and we get a good firework display every night from the German Lines with different coloured flare lights, things which we very seldom use, for our lines are always in darkness. I think that the Hun is always expecting an attack, what a blessing it will be when it is all finished. [...]
I Remain Your Loving Bro Sam

JUNE 21st 1918 IN FRANCE

Dear Bro and Sister,

In answer to your letter of June 13th which I received while in the trenches, I was very pleased to hear from you but so sorry to hear of Redvers being so ill. It is the same as you say he would be doing the country far more good if they had let him stay at his work, instead they have took him away only for him to go into hospital where he is simply a burden and expense to the country. But they do not seem to care about that, all they want is men, no matter whether they are fit or not. It seems hard to say but it would serve them right if he was never able to follow the duties of a soldier, he is far better where he is than being out here where there is nothing but danger and hardships. Then you say that you have heard from Bro Willie and that he is going on alright but not getting enough to eat which I know is very hard to bear but I am pleased to say that we are not very often like that although some days we only get two and a half biscuits per day and these are the times that you hear the men swear, but to take the men on the whole, the troubles they have to go through and the thoughts of home, they are a cheerful lot, it is very seldom that they are downhearted and they always grumble most when the rations are short. So you say that the garden is set and all that you want is some rain for the making of a good crop. Well these last two days we have had a good drop out here and it makes it very awkward walking in the Trenches where you are soon covered in mud for the ground out here is very chalky and it sticks like glue to you. Then it has turned very cold also and you have to stand all night on duty watching the Germans for you never know when he is going to attack. We get the most of our sleep during the day for we are not afraid of the Beast coming over the top for he knows if he did he would have a poor chance of reaching our lines, without paying a heavy sacrifice for ours is a strong position. There has been a lot of heavy firing both on our left and right and I heard that we had made a slight advance on the left. This last two or three mornings somewhere about four o'clock we have had a visit from a German Airman, so it gave us all the chance of a bit of rifle practice in shooting at him, but sorry to say we did not bring him down, but never mind, better luck next time. I shall be only be too pleased to have a bit of garden of my own when I get back again which I hope to some day, although at the time of writing there seems very small hopes of that happening yet awhile but one never knows what may happen, we can only hope for the best and trust in one above. [...] I Remain your loving Bro Sam.

JULY 1st 1918 IN FRANCE

Dear Bro and Sister,

[…] No doubt you will be wondering why I have not wrote before now but I'm pleased to say that it is no fault of mine. You see we have been travelling again, the first part of the journey we did in motor lorries and even some of the London Omnibuses and I rode in one of them. We were riding about 9 hours. Then we broke our journey and stayed for a day and a night in a French Village where we were bombed during the night, but pleased to say that no harm was done. The next day we started on a march to reach our destination, we were all done up before we got there for it was a very hot day and the roads were dry and dusty. We were all pleased when we got there. [...] Last night, our first night in this camp, we had the German planes over us again dropping bombs, it is awful for your nerves, you can hear them circling round then down comes a bomb, and you keep wondering if it is going to be your turn. After they had gone we were shelled by the Germans and I can tell you that you get very little sleep. I only wish that it was finished and I was back home again. [...] I remain your loving Bro Sam

JULY 6th 1918 IN BELGIUM

Dear Bro and Sister,

[…] I am sure that I cannot understand why it is that sometimes it takes a letter a matter of 10 days to reach you, there must be some neglect somewhere but it is not for us to complain. This letter that I have just received from you has taken nine days to reach me but I expect the cause of that is through us being on the move. We have gone a good many miles from the last place, still going the same direction that I spoke of. Have seen a few American Soldiers today for the first time. I must say that they are very large men, but they do not seem very lively, no doubt they are a little shy, which I expect will not last very long. [...]

You wish no more than I do as regards Hospitals but it does not seem my luck, nothing seems to ail me, I only wish something would for I am tired of this life, how I wish this war would end and I was back again in Civil Life. So you are wanting some rain, or else you will not have a very good potato crop, it is the same out here, everything is dry and dusty and I am sure that rain would do a lot of good. I am very pleased that you have sent a few envelopes for all mine got stuck when I was in the Trenches, pleased to say that we have plenty of writing paper but anytime it gets short I will let you know. Yes it was very good of the people of Glasgow sending these things which they very often do, it must be very expensive. [...] I remain your loving Bro Sam.

PS I trust that none of my previous letters have upset any of you [...]

JULY 9th 1918 IN FRANCE

Dear Bro and Sister,

[...] I have been in a few countries since I left home but I find no place like Blighty. Pleased to hear of Bro Will being home on leave, I only wish it would be my luck to get home but we shall have to hope for the best, but sunny days will come again. [...] We are under canvas now away from the firing line close to a large town doing some training. There are a lot of Americans out here now, when we pass them on the march we shout to them "Hello Sammy" they reply with "Hello Jock" they are a fine body of men but appear to be on the slow side, but I think that if they get the same training as we get they will soon improve.

Very pleased to say that we have very good rations and plenty of them. You hear very little grumbling now for every man gets plenty to eat although I have seen the time when we had not enough to eat. I have done a little more travelling have been in another country, but back again in France, do not know how long we shall be in this camp - might move any moment. [...] Wishing you all the best of health and Good Luck, hoping to meet you all again some day. Your loving Bro Sam

JULY 14th 1918 IN BELGIUM

Dear Bro and Sister,

[...] This last week we have been away in the country training, we were in tents and we all enjoyed the change very much, it was a lovely country about that camp then there were two or three small villages close to us. I had a look round them, me and another young man used to have a walk at night, there was also a large town very near to us but I only saw it when marching through it. We have left that place now and gone into a fresh one where we are to get more training, we are still in tents and I can assure you that they are very healthy to live in. We have had a lot of rain this last day or two and it has done heaps of good to the crops for they wanted rain very badly, I suppose you are the same in Blighty. I shall be glad when it comes my turn for a leave, for I am longing to see you all and the good old home - the best place in the world. I am pleased to say that we are getting good rations and I hope and trust you are doing so, for when you are getting plenty to eat you feel more content. [...] I only wish the war would come to an end and we were all back home again, what rejoicing there would be but it is the same as you say we shall have to trust in one above and hope for the best. [...] I Remain Your Loving Bro Sam

JULY 21st 1918 IN FRANCE

Dear Bro and Sister,

[...]You must not be surprised if you do not hear from me as often as usual for it is no fault of mine, you see, we are always on the move, we have covered a good many miles this week and still going on. I have seen [censored, probably CHANTILLY] race course which is a very fine one [...]. I am writing this letter in a little village where the Huns were two or three days ago, but the Yanks and the French chased them away from it. There was a lot of Hun Prisoners of War we passed on the way. The scenery about here is very beautiful, it makes me think of Matlock. Yes, you told me all about the accident at Chilwell, I was sorry to see how many lost their lives. Let them know at home about me moving about, and me not being able to write as often as I would like to. [...]
Your Loving Bro Sam

The letter dated 21st July was the last letter from Sam which his family received. He was killed on 29th July 1918. The Regimental records say as follows:

"8th SCOTTISH RIFLES JULY 23rd TO JULY 29th 1918

Our reports show that in the last week of July 1918 the 8th Scottish Rifles were among the British regiments who co-operated with the French in the Marne offensive, which proved to be the beginning of victory for the Allies. On July 18th the French began to move forward on a 27-mile front and two days later the Germans were forced to re-cross the river Marne. On July 23rd there was fierce fighting throughout the sector and the 8th Scottish Rifles suffered casualties in what one man calls "the Soissons battle when we were supporting the French". One incidence is described as follows :

"On July 23rd we had just arrived at our position on the Marne front and had dug in. A shell came over about 10 yards away from me and killed or wounded about a dozen men. This was about 7am. For the next 6 days little progress seems to have been made and on July 29th another hotly contested action took place. One man says "we were advancing at a village near Soissons but were held up by machine gun fire. Some men got into some high growing corn and have not been heard of since. My company dug in".

Another gives a few more details "We were attacking near Soissons and had men killed by machine gun bullets in the open. We had to retire at 4.30pm and the dead were left. We recovered the ground 2 or 3 days afterwards". It is clear that in such a desperate struggle as this, men have little opportunity to note or record the fate of their comrades".

The 'Cross of Sacrifice' was designed by Sir Reginald Blomfield and is usually present in Commonwealth war cemeteries containing 40 or more graves. It is normally a limestone Latin cross ranging in height from 18 to 32 feet. On the face of the cross is a bronze broadsword, blade down. The Cross represents the faith of the majority of the dead and the sword represents the military character of the cemetery. This one is at the Loos Memorial.

150

Sam's sister made extended enquiries even into 1920 to try to establish the location of his body and there are many letters from various official authorities in response to her letters to them. The family have always believed that he was one of the men who was attacking through the high growing corn.

A letter dated 29th May 1919 from the Director of Graves Registration, War Office, St James Square, London reads as follows:

"Dear Madam, in reply to your letter of 19th May 1919 I regret that I can only repeat my letter of 28th January 1919 in which I stated that Private S Kidger is reported to be buried in the vicinity of Beugneux on the left side of wood to Servenay SSE of Soissons. You may rest assured that if when my officers are working in this area they are able to locate the grave so that it can be registered in this office, I will at once write to you again, but until this has been done it is impossible for a photograph to be taken. Signed for Major General Director G.C.R.& E."

We understand nothing more was heard and Sam is listed as missing with no known grave. His name is on the war memorials at Ilkeston and at Soissons.

His name is also recorded in the book of fatalities in the Regimental Museum of the Cameronians in Edinburgh Castle.

United Methodist Churches – Ilkeston Circuit Magazine
[Transcribed by Gary Henshaw]

[January 1915] **NEWS OF THE CHURCHES - South Street** The year [1914] closes with several items of interest. We have had visits from our boys who are engaged in the King's service, and they have had a warm welcome. Lieutenant N. Dexter has spent his Christmas at home, and our esteemed friend, Mrs. Riley, has her naval and army representatives (now 3 in number) to cheer her Christmastide. Corporal Spencer has also been with us, and these warriors have not forgotten the sanctuary at South Street. If others have been here we have not heard their names mentioned, but we are not unmindful of them. We hear a rumour that our friend Naylor is in hospital, but await confirmation, hoping that our fears will be falsified. [...]

Nottingham Road YOUNG MEN IN CAMP – the doings and whereabouts of the young men of Nottm. Road who have enlisted in the army will be followed with kindly and anxious concern. [...] We were delighted to see them looking so fit and well when at home on a few days furlough. At a Church Meeting held recently, it was decided to send each of the young men a Book of Services and Prayers compiled specially for soldiers and sailors. [...] In a letter to us Rifleman John Beaumont expresses his thanks for the kindness of so many friends at home. He requests the prayers of the friends not only for himself but for all other young men who have been called from home. Now in the midst of the temptations of camp life, he feels more than ever the value of the teachings he has received in the Sunday School. Gunner Joe Stirland also thanks the many Kimberley friends who have been kind to him. Every Sunday he attends the United Methodist Church. [...] Private Bert Ginniver sends his kind regards to all the friends. Just now he says "our condition is not enviable, we are sleeping in a barn, and up to the boot tops in mud." Running through the letters of all the young men is a sincere appreciation of any kindness shown to them by the friends at home. Well - the best we can wish for is that the war may soon come to an end, and that they may return home safely.

[March 1915] **South Street** [...] Letters conveying good wishes have been received from Lieutenant N. Lloyd Dexter, Corporal A. Spencer [...] Private Cecil Stout, who is stationed in Norfolk, joins in these kindly expressions.

David Hudson

A postcard sent by newly joined Rifleman Digby Hudson to his family from
Larkhill Camp in Wiltshire before leaving for the front.

[May 1915] **Awsworth** Mr. Sisson had to attend the funeral of his brother, Mr. Berwick [Bewick?] Sisson of Cotmanhay, who bravely fought and fell in the battle of Neuve Chapelle. The sympathy of the choir and friends was more deeply felt than expressed for Mr. A Sisson on this occasion.

[July 1915] **South Street** *In Memoriam* PRIVATE ROY NAYLOR [q.v.] an old South Street Scholar, having been killed in action, a memorial service was held in the South Street Church on Sunday May 30th, conducted by the Rev Jas. Stephens. Our departed brother was in the R.A.M.C., and the body of the church was filled with members of the Local Ambulance Corps, who attended with their band. The roll of honour was hung below the pulpit, also a chaplet of laurel leaves, sent by the Sunday School, with a card containing the words "In memory of one of our brave boys." The family of mourners were present, also the scholars of the Sunday School. The Rev Jas. Stephens, in his address, referred to the noble character of the fallen hero, and the fine testimony paid by the officers to the service so valiantly rendered the Cause of Liberty on the fields of France. Private Henry Mallen, who fell in the Canadian ranks, had also been connected with our school in years past, and sympathetic references were made, during the service, to his self sacrifice. The service was very impressive and concluded with a funeral march, effectively rendered on the organ by Mr. Evans.

[October 1915] **South Street** [...] With profound sorrow we learn of the death from wounds, on October 15th, of Rifleman Henry Wilkinson, of the King's Royal Rifles. He was the eldest son of Mr. and Mrs. Isaac Wilkinson, of Little Hallam. On March 18th he enlisted, and went to France about three months ago. He was wounded in the severe fighting towards the end of last month, sustaining injuries in the head. Our hearts go out in deepest sympathy to his mother, who is a member of the Women's Pleasant Hour, and to the family, in this sad hour.

Memories of 1914
Ilkeston man in a 'Telegraph' picture
Derby Daily Telegraph, Friday 15th November 1929

Much interest was taken in the photograph of a sentry on duty outside the Guildhall in Derby during the war which the "Derby Daily Telegraph" published in the special Armistice Day number on Monday. Many must have wondered who the sentry was, and if he was later killed in the war. He wasn't. He is very much alive and is none other than Mr Herbert Chester Spibey (37) of Jackson's-avenue, Ilkeston. Mr Spibey is known to many Derbyshire people as he is groundsman at Ilkeston County Cricket Ground. "I was very much surprised when shown the 'Telegraph' containing my photo" said Mr Spibey to a "Derby Daily Telegraph" reporter. "I remembered in a moment that I had not seen the photo since shortly after it was taken, in the first week of the war. I was in camp with the 'B' (Ilkeston) Company of the Sherwood Foresters when war broke out. We came home on a Sunday, and were called to the Stanton-road Drill Hall Ilkeston on the Monday, and instructed what to get ready, and marched to Derby on the Tuesday. I remember we billeted in the Athenaeum Rooms. I was put on guard either the same day or on Wednesday or Thursday, and I recollect the photographer snapping me as one of the very first men (if not the first) on sentry-go outside a public building in Derby. I never thought I would see the photo in the 'Telegraph' after all these years! Strangely enough, it was the only time I was on guard as a private, for I was promoted sergeant almost immediately".

Mr Spibey was badly wounded at Gommecourt in the Battle of the Somme in 1916. He was then taken prisoner, and after being interned in Germany and Holland did not get home till after the Armistice.

Attentive readers will note that the Telegraph mis-spelt Hubert Chester Spiby's name.

153

Sam Straw's letters transcribed by Margaret Richardson

January 4, 1915   xxxx   write back and tell me how
you are getting on please

     XXXXXXXX for ivy

I will write again soon.

Dear Mother & Children,

    Just a few lines hoping to find you well and in the pink as it leaves
your son quite well at presant. I received your parcel quite safe this
morning and everythink was a treat which made me jump with joy when I saw
the pies and apples and the lard - they all came as a surprise and today,
Monday, I stuffed myself a treat at tea-time and my pal was put on sentry
duty as I came off, so I gave him a bit of lard and some pie which will
help him to get through the nights work. The night I was on it rained and
snowed like the old lad but I was quite warm but my feet which I got warm
later. Now mother what do you think of Bob haveing to go. It as quite got
my rag out. I will tell you the reason why, their is all the swanks
walking up & down the streets and will not come and do their bit while they
keep on fetching the poor people to do everythink and them in the finish
they will perhaps be no better thought of than those who have stoped behind
but as the old saying is, we shall have to wait and see but it has been
hard on a good many poor people the same as yourself but now they have
started to fetch them I should had to a gone so it is happen the best I
came at first. We shall have to think that way for their is nothink else
for it, the good old pit lads will make somebody look round befor we have
done so good night mother and children, wishing you all good luck, till
your loveing son Samuel returns.

Sunday, 12 December, 1915

Dear Mother,

    Just a few lines in answer to your letter and parcel I received quite
safe yesterday. Hopeing this will find you all in the best of health as it
leaves me in the pink at presant. My word, you did not forget to pack the
parcel this time round, it would not have got smashed up if it had been put
under a steamroller. I was very pleased with it, and you must have gone to
a lot of trouble in getting the things together. I have use for everythink
for its not very often that I go out when we are out of the trenches, for
their is not much round this part of the world to interest anyone. We are
able to get a drink of beer but it is no bottle, it would take a month for
anyone to get drunk on this stuff but it will do for the time being. The
letter I received yesterday was the one sent by Fred and I will answer it
sometime next week. I have send one to Louie but I had not got the parcel
at the time I wrote it so will you please tell her that I have got it when
she comes home. I hope you are all getting on alright and just see that
little ivy gets her stocking full this Xmas. I hope you will all make
yourselves as happy as you can and live in hope that the next Xmas will be
better still and that I shall spend it with you. We can't come this year,
for the old savage tribe want a bit of looking after and we should not like
them to get out of hand after all the trouble. Now mother dear, let me
thank all those of you once more for the parcel and I hope you all spend a
good time and all enjoy good health this Xmas. Please remember me to Freds
young lady and I hope I shall be able to see both mine and the latest
recruit to the family so now I will bid you all good day and good luck for
I am still your old Son Samuel.

I will write again soon.   Born 1892
                                 still going strong

                    Ivy XXXXX

     C & H XXXXX   Mother XXXXX

October 23, 1915

Dear Mother & Sister,

        Just a few lines hopeing to find you well as it leaves me quite well
at presant. I received your letter today, Friday, at tea which cheered me
up very much. I was beginning to think you had forgot me when I got it. I
am very pleased with Graces photo which is a very good one but I shall have
to send it back because I have nowere to put it. I had my photo taken at
the front of the lent(?) with the other chaps and if I can get one I will
send you one at once. I have got my new cloths and when I get paid for the
old ones which will be 6/- I will send you the lot, perhaps it will be next
week which I hope it will be so I have been vaxenated again today Friday
and by stars it does make the arm ache but it will be alright in a day or
to. Now my old ducks, do your best for Xmas and we will see what I have
got to tell you then Dear Mother and sister, you know that anybody that
listed at the time of this war will always be thought a lot of and their is
as much worries for you two as their is for me and as soon as the war is
over I sharnt be long befor I am at home and anybody that tells you that I
shall have to stop three years, they are telling lies. Them that is here
knows more than those who is boggers who like to hear their taungs wag so
don't get downhearted for I think that the war will be over by Xmas and let
us hope so. Now my ducks I will close my letter so that I can chuck the
post. See after my little Ivy for me till I come home and if anybody puts
a finger on her I will pull their eyes out. So good night and god bless
you all from your ever loveing brother and son, Sambo

21st February 1916

Dear Mrs. Straw,

        I am grieved to tell you that your son L.S. Straw, 158862, 11th
Sherwood Foresters, has been wounded in the right shoulder and spine.

        He was admitted here, No. 2 Casualty Clearing Station, B & F France,
this morning. Owing to the wound of the spine his lower limbs are
paralysed, and it is too soon yet to tell how far he may recover the use of
them.

        As he can travel in a hospital train, we shall send him to the base
tomorrow and he will let you know what hospital he gets sent to there.

        I am distressed to have to give you such bad news of your son, and to
think of all your anxiety. You may be quite sure that everything possible
will be done for him.

        Believe me to be,

                Yours very truly,

                M.E. Vernon Harcourt
                Sister

155

Fred Karno's Army

A marching song, very popular with the 'New Army' and conscripts:

> *We are Fred Karno's Army, the ragtime Infantry,*
> *We cannot march, we cannot shoot, what b***** use are we?*
> *And when we get to Berlin, the Kaiser he will say*
> *"Hoch Hoch! Mein Gott! What a b***** fine lot!*
> *Fred Karno's Infantry"*

(Tune : "The Church's one foundation")

Author's note : Fred Karno was a Music-Hall impresario whose troupe in the early 1900's included Charlie Chaplin and Stan Laurel. There are a number of variations to the wording, very few of which would be printable here ...

Anne Cook

AFTERWORD
1st July 1986;
Finding Uncle Henry

Seventy years after the local territorials from the 1/5 Sherwood Foresters went 'over the top' my father and my 21 year old self embarked on our first trip to the battlefield of the Somme. It was a bit of an adventure; in these days before the internet and with him having little or no French my Dad had asked a friend (Kath Trueman) to make reservations over the telephone with the owners of a café in the large village of Pas-en-Artois for our first two nights. Neither of us had driven in France before; you had to paint your headlights yellow and there were all sorts of worrying differences with driving over there - odd priority at junctions and strange things happening on roundabouts.

We crossed the channel on the ferry (no alternative in those days) and had a good journey on almost deserted autoroutes in the sunshine. On the way across country from the motorway we began to notice first one then as our eyes knew what to look for many small enclosures dotted around the rolling landscape. The most prominent feature of each was a large white stone cross and the walled enclosure was covered with stark white headstones and bright green grass. They varied in size and design from just a dozen or so markers to many lines of them and these appeared almost at random through a landscape uninterrupted by hedgerows. Very often they were reached by a little used track across a dry field; the soil was poor and chalky. They had almost no relationship to the modern roads.

We stopped, of course. The problem was that having stopped for one it felt disrespectful not to stop for the next. Each immaculately smart cemetery had a brass-doored box in the gatepost behind which was a register of all those buried with short details of who they had been. There was also a visitors book and even the most remote of the small cemeteries seemed to have been visited recently by some of the many Brits over for the seventieth anniversary. A cameraderie developed between all of us foreigners; the occupants of almost all the British registered cars we passed gave a friendly wave and had a few words with us at the frequent stops.

Despite all this cheeriness, we arrived at our pleasant little café in a sober mood and ready for a drink. The young owners were very friendly and with my schoolboy French we managed to communicate. They spoke little English. It turned out that his grandfather had been killed at Verdun. The front of the café seemed to be filled with Frenchmen straight out of central casting, complete with Gauloises, berets and vests. They seemed to shrug a lot. I liked it.

That evening we went out to find Uncle Henry. My father had been named after his father's older brother who had died on the first day of the Battle of the Somme in what some people don't regard as part of the battle proper at all - the 'diversionary attack' on Gommecourt. Foncquevillers was on the British front line opposite Gommecourt some five hundred yards away, held by the Germans. 21 year old Lewis Gunner Henry Shaw had died not long after 7.30am on Saturday 1st July 1916 on a glorious Summer morning somewhere in no man's land along with many others from Ilkeston on the worst day the British Army ever had.

30th June / 1st July 1986 :
Finding Uncle Henry

Foncquevillers Military Cemetery Gates,
the Register and the author aged 21 in 1986.
Below :
Veterans at the 70th Anniversary commemoration;
frail but determined to pay their respects.

Following some of the new green Commonwealth War Graves signs we drove up a farm track past barns and cows until the trees parted and on the left we saw the cemetery. Not the most beautiful one we saw that trip, but just as perfectly turned out, as if it had been completed seven years ago rather than seventy.

We found Henry's grave in the middle of a long row towards the rear of the cemetery. We saw that most of this row of headstones had three names not one and wondered why this would be. Reading his epitaph "My darling boy. Fought the good fight, and is rewarded in Heaven. Love Mother" my father remembered his grandmother, who had died when he was just eight years old but had made the trip to this grave before he was born. We had brought some flowers and as the sun set slowly on that warm summer evening we laid them there.

Early the next day we walked through the cemetery again, wondering at the stories behind the brief few lines on each headstone. Plenty of young men who died on the same day. Chinese labourers. Flyers from the Second World War, shot down near here. And Captain John Leslie Green MD VC, the 1/5 Sherwood Foresters' dedicated young Medical Officer who had been posthumously awarded a Victoria Cross for his work out in no man's land that day.

As we were leaving it struck me that I was the same age as Henry had been then; 21. He had started work as a miner at 13, joined the territorials before the war and fought in the trenches for over a year including at the Battle of Loos in 1915. And what had I done? Our lives could not have been more different but despite this I have always felt a connection to my great uncle and visit his grave whenever I can.

The next day we went to the official commemoration at the huge Thiepval Memorial to the Missing, a landmark for miles around designed by Sir Edwin Lutyens - the architect of the Cenotaph in Whitehall. The great and the good were there (The Duke of Kent, the Defence Secretary, the local Prefect, some other politicians) along with several veterans, rather frail but still keen to show their respect for fallen comrades. Very many members of the public were there too, from all over Britain and further afield. There was a large contingent from Northern Ireland and also several French veterans with their tricolour banners. A piper played 'The Flowers of the Forest' under the arch - goose bumps all round and you could hear a pin drop. I can never hear that music without thinking of that moment. I was there ten years later and have been to the service a number of times since. My father and I were also there eighteen years after that first service on the day when a splendid new visitor centre was dedicated.

Until that day in 1986 it had all been a bit abstract; just some history. That visit made it very personal. I wanted to know more about these men and what made them do what they did and how they lived. It gave me an interest in the war which has lasted, on and off, for nearly thirty years and eventually led to this book.

Grant Shaw
May, 2014

Joe Ellaby

Part of Joseph Daniel Ellaby's long photograph of no-man's land, somewhere to the north-east of Arras towards the end of the War.

Borough of Ilkeston.

THE GREAT WAR, 1914 TO 1919.

Official Celebration of the Treaty of Peace,

SATURDAY, 19th JULY, 1919.

_____

Reception given by the Mayor (Alderman Arthur Henshaw, J.P.) to welcome Demobilized Sailors and Soldiers, on the Pimlico Recreation Ground, at 4 p.m.

Mr. W. Button

GOD SAVE THE KING.

161

Annie Eyre, a local VAD (Voluntary Aid Detachment) Nurse.
Some of these volunteers served on the Western Front.
Famous VADs include novelists Vera Brittain and Agatha Christie,
aviator Amelia Earhart and explorer Freya Stark.

These greetings cards, embroidered with silk were a popular gift from the front
to loved ones back in 'Blighty'.

These interesting images were taken from a family photo album inherited by Hazel Hartshorn.
Unfortunately, there is no indication as to the names of those pictured.

THE FINAL WORD

A community publication such as this relies on volunteers and submissions from the public, in this case relatives of those who served. Sometimes recollections and family stories can dim or get brighter with the passing of the years and we have done our best to verify the information which has been kindly supplied to us. Likewise, although the rise of the internet has meant that more information than ever before is available to the researcher, you are rarely looking at the primary sources of that information but instead rely on others who have transcribed, with varying degrees of accuracy, the original information into digital form.

We are sorry if any errors have inadvertently crept in to the 'facts' which we have printed in this book and if you have evidence to the contrary then do please let us know so that we may correct our own records for future use.

If you have any stories, memorabilia or particularly photographs of any local people who served abroad in the Great War, we would still be interested to see and copy them for any future publication.

Please email **mail@ilkestonhistory.org.uk**

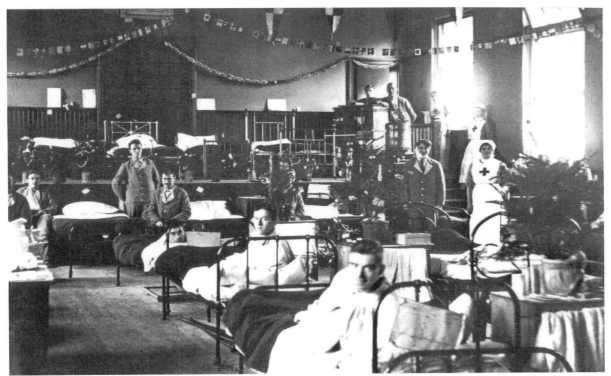

St Mary's Schoolrooms at Ilkeston were used as a hospital for convalescing troops during the war.　　　Erewash Museum

ABOUT ILKESTON & DISTRICT LOCAL HISTORY SOCIETY

The Society was established in 1966 to encourage the study of all aspects of the local history of Ilkeston and the surrounding area, and to publish this information for the benefit of the public.

The Society has an active programme of visits and talks on a varied range of subjects and meets regularly at least once a month in Ilkeston.

We also publish books and pamphlets on different aspects of social, industrial and family history with a connection to the locality. New members and enquiries, both regarding membership and on any local history related subject are always welcome.

More information about us, our activities and much about Ilkeston's history is on our ever-expanding website at **www.ilkestonhistory.org.uk**.

Also recently published by the Society :

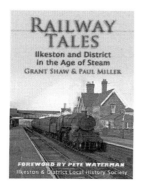

Railway Tales - Ilkeston & District in the Age of Steam
by Grant Shaw and Paul Miller (2012) (£10)

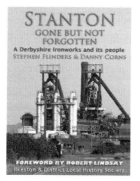

Stanton - Gone but not Forgotten
by Stephen Flinders and Danny Corns (2013) (£10)

Email **mail@ilkestonhistory.org.uk** for mail order prices on these and our many other publications, including our popular series of historical maps of Ilkeston.

INDEX of those whose stories or images feature in this book

A 'Khaki Wedding'. Miss Ellen Selina Wright (centre, right) married Fred Shaw (centre left) in 1919.

Fred has not been demobbed yet so he still wears his uniform with pride. He went on to become a fairly well respected local artist in the 1940's and 1950's. Nell was a great friend to the author when he was a child; she died in 1977. Her mother Martha Wright (the author's great-grandmother) sits to her left and sister Gwen (the author's grandmother) sits at Fred's knee along with sister Beryl, also in white. These last two also appear in the photo of brother Victor in Chapter 2. Nell's brother George Arthur Wright (standing behind her) went on to be Mayor of Ilkeston in 1950.